Bristol Temple Meads East: the train has come in from the South Wales relief line and is directed to Platform 1 or 2. The train engine is a 'Hall' and the leading one is a 'Grange', possibly No 6838 *Goodmoor Grange*. The Midland line is almost exactly obscured by steam from the engines. Note, beyond the gantry of Great Western colour-light signals, the huge number of coaches in the Kingsland Road sidings.
G. F. Heiron

FROM THE FOOTPLATE

DEVONIAN
– BRADFORD TO PAIGNTON

STEPHEN AUSTIN

IAN ALLAN
Publishing

Cover:
The 'Devonian' with a pair of 'Jubilee' class 4-6-0s in charge blasts out of Wickwar Tunnel. *From a painting by George F Heiron.*

First published 1994

ISBN 0 7110 2229 1

Published by Ian Allan Publishing

an imprint of Ian Allan Ltd, Terminal House, Station Approach, Shepperton, Surrey TW17 8AS.
Printed by Ian Allan Printing Ltd, Coombelands House, Coombelands Lane, Addlestone, Weybridge, Surrey KT15 1HY.

Title page
From the footplate; heading down to the west on a beautiful spring day, 3 May 1957. The photographer is on No 4960 *Pyle Hall* passing Whiteball Tunnel down distant and about to enter the tunnel. *Kenneth Leech*

Below:
The northbound 'Devonian', train No 240, running into Derby Midland over London Road Junction on 28 July 1951. The engine, No 45561 *Saskatchewan*, has an old-style tender and the layout is still controlled by Midland lower-quadrant signals. *A. N. Yeates*

Contents

Preface

It seems as though there is hardly any feature of our railway system that does not have books about it in plenty, but most of them are detailed close studies of one topic which, with no disrespect, are unlikely to attract the lay reader. Conversely, there is, so far as I know, no general guide book on, or history of, this country that gives railways more than a dismissive sentence or two. Therefore, to communicate to more people the fascination of the steam engine and the way it is used, what is wanted is a broad-based presentation of the railway in the landscape, the engine on the railway and the men on the engine, doing what they are there to do — running trains — and that is the intention of this little book. If more knowledgeable readers feel it lacks depth, I hope they can relax and enjoy it as an excursion, and if anyone feels 'technical' subjects are not their line, I hope they will find a description not just of machines but of some highly skilled craftsmen doing a demanding job in a vital role of service to the community. Written 36 years after the period in which it is set, it is obviously nostalgic and no apology is made, or deemed necessary, for being so. Not everything done in the past was worse than what we have now.

The absence of women from these pages is not discriminatory, but merely a reflection of the way things were run in 1957. The practice of describing engines as feminine, frowned on by some, is a just allusion to their power, vitality and beauty. The sketches, whilst double-checked where possible, are mine and the errors are mine also. The narrative content is not intended to refer to any specific people or events.

It is my pleasure to acknowledge the information sources, which fall into three categories. For most of the data on railway working I am indebted to the Public Record Office, and for local details I thank the staff of the public libraries of Bradford, Leeds, Birmingham, Bromsgrove, Bristol, Newton Abbot and Torquay. Further inspiration has come from the Bass Museum and the Bristol Industrial Museum.

Of the many books available, I would particularly recommend *Rail Centres: Leeds-Bradford* by Stephen R. Batty, *Rail Centres: Bristol* by Colin Maggs, *Railways in Burton* by H. N. Twells, *The Midland in Gloucestershire* by Peter Smith, *The Newton Abbot to Kingswear Railway* by C.R. Potts, *Rails Along the Sea Wall* by Peter Kay, *The Lickey Incline* by H. C. Casserley, the *Handbook of BR Steam Motive Power Depots* by Paul Smith, the *British Association Guide to Leeds*, the *Shell Guides*, *Locomotive Management* by Jas. T. Hodgson & Chas. S. Lake, *British Locomotive Types* by the Railway Publishing Co, *A Journey to the Heart of England* by C. Hillier, *Portrait of Somerset* by Bryan Little, *Summer Saturdays in the West* by David St. J. Thomas & S. Rocksborough-Smith, *GWR Engines* by W. G. Chapman, *Glorious Devon* by S. P. B. Mais, the David & Charles Regional Histories on the West Midlands by Rex Christiansen and South & West Yorkshire by David Joy, a feature article on the Birmingham-Bristol line by G. Freeman Allan in the 1957 *Trains Illustrated, Taunton Steam* by Colin Maggs, the RCH Handbook and of course Williams' *Midland Railway*.

Thirdly, thanks to those who have provided hospitality and facilities: Paul & Mary Twine, Sheena Mackenzie, Mr & Mrs Irving, the Great Central Railway, the Great Western Society and Ian Allan Publishing's own library. I also thank Mr G. W. Morrison, Mr R. M. Casserley, Mr A. J. Somers, Mr Bryan Gibson, Mr K. Field, Mr D. Fish and Mr Chris Austin. And the biggest thank-you of all is to my sister, Mrs Janet Price, who has been my support throughout.

Stephen Austin
Ewell
March 1994

Devonian

The Devonian Train No. 251

Bradford Forster Square	d 9.50am		Up direction
Shipley	a 9.56	d 9.57	
Guiseley Jn	9.58		Slow Line
Leeds City North	a 10.12	d 10.20	
Altofts Jn	10.35		
Normanton	10.37		
Cudworth	10.56		
Wath Road Jn	11.8		
Rotherham Masborough	11.15		
Sheffield Midland	a 11.23	d 11.29	Fast Line
Dore & Totley	11.40		
Dronfield	11.45		
Chesterfield Midland	a 11.51	d 11.53	
Clay Cross	11.59		
Stretton	12.5 pm		
Ambergate	12.13		Avoiding Line
Derby Midland	a 12.25	d 12.30	Down direction
Stenson Jn	12.37		
Burton upon Trent	12.44		
Wichnor Jn	12.51		
Tamworth	1.0		
Kingsbury	1.7		Fast Line
Water Orton	1.11		
Saltley	1.17		
Birmingham New Street	a 1.22	d 1.30	
Selly Oak	1.38		
Blackwell	1.49		
Bromsgrove	1.54		
Dunhampstead	2.1		
Abbots Wood Jn	2.7		
Ashchurch	2.18		
Cheltenham Lansdown	a 2.29	d 2.34	
Lansdown Jn	2.35		
Gloucester Eastgate	a 2.45	d 2.51	
Standish Jn	3.1		
Berkeley Road	3.10		
Yate	3.22		
Mangotsfield	3.28		10min recovery
Bristol Temple Meads East	3.45		
Bristol Temple Meads	a 3.47	d 4.0	Main Line
Bristol West Depot	4.5		
Worle Jn	4.23		
Weston-super-Mare	a 4.27	d 4.30	
Uphill Jn	4.34		
Highbridge	4.45		
Bridgwater	a 4.53	d 4.55	Main Line from Cogload Jn
Taunton	a 5.13	d 5.18	Main Line
Whiteball Tunnel	5.37		
Cowley Bridge Jn	5.55		
Exeter St David's	a 5.59	d 6.4	
Dawlish	a 6.22	d 6.24	
Teignmouth	a 6.30	d 6.32	
Newton Abbot	a 6.42	d 6.51	
Aller Jn	6.54		
Torre	a 7.3	d 7.5	
Torquay	a 7.7	d 7.10	
Paignton	a 7.15	d 7.25	ecs
Churston	a 7.33	d 7.37	
Kingswear	a 7.45		

Devonian

Preamble

Glorious Devon! The phrase has come to mean an image of leafy lanes, pretty villages and blue seas; a place fashioned, so the guide-books say, solely for the delight of the visitor; a siren luring us from our drear industrial towns. In the mid-1990s, when these words are being written, the average holidaymaker's view of Devon comprises the backs of lorries and a succession of CAR PARK FULL notices — hardly the basis for an armchair excursion of pleasure. Instead, let us travel in the year 1957, when the lanes and villages are still quiet even when the county is hosting masses of visitors, because most of them arrive by train.

One of the many trains linking the grimy mills to the golden beaches is the 'Devonian', the 9.50am Bradford Forster Square-Paignton service.

This is a long journey of 324.5 miles, fetching up in Paignton at 7.15pm — 9hr 25min in all. There are 18 intermediate stops which total 87min, so the running time is 7hr 48min, an average speed of 41.6mph. On Saturdays the northbound train starts from Kingswear, and on Friday evenings the southbound train runs empty from Paignton to Kingswear, increasing the distance to 331 miles.

The journey will be more enjoyable if we make it on a weekday, because summer Saturdays have become really too much of a good thing. In 1957 passenger travel on British Railways has reached its highest level ever, following the previous year's petrol rationing, a bus strike this summer and a demand from an increasingly prosperous populace for holiday travel. The West Country is taking the full weight of this deluge and the railway is overloaded on Saturdays, culminating in the busiest day ever on 27 July. Coaches, which only run on half a dozen days in the year, are brought out of their sidings to form dozens of extra trains. The resultant congestion ends up with disgruntled passengers delivered up to three hours late at their resorts, and harassed controllers trying to find crews for trains and vice versa. This overwork is not like 'staying late at the office';

it is no fun being told to do another two hours' firing at the end of a long, hot day, or finishing work a hundred miles from home without knowing how you are to get back. No wonder tempers tend to wear a little thin.

The railways have always done their best to spread this undesirable travel peak. Indeed, the very first guides to Devon and Cornwall attractions extolled their virtues as winter resorts. Another point easily overlooked about trains like the 'Devonian' is that, while they terminate at holiday resorts, they also form part of the service connecting the industrial centres of Leeds, Sheffield, Derby, Birmingham, et al. For most of the year that is far more important than the great Saturday exodus.

The second-class return fare to Paignton is £4 16s 8d from Leeds, £4 5s from Sheffield, £1 16s 8d from Bristol. You can have your luggage collected and delivered at 5s per case. Bicycles, prams and dogs are charged at single fare for a return journey. Luncheon costs 8s 6d, or you may obtain a packed lunch from the refreshment room at Bradford, Leeds, Sheffield, Chesterfield, Derby, Birmingham, Cheltenham, Gloucester or Bristol. When you reach the West Country you may buy unlimited travel for seven days on a variety of Holiday Runabout tickets; a typical one, covering Exeter to Totnes, Ashburton, Moretonhampstead and Kingswear, costing 17s 6d.

The 'Devonian' is essentially a Midland Railway train. That statement may seem surprising, since that company ceased its independent existence 34 years ago and, if it comes to that, had been incorporated into the London, Midland & Scottish Railway before the title 'Devonian' came into use in 1927. However, the proof of it lies in the fact that the service uses Forster Square station, the terminus of the Leeds & Bradford Railway (taken over by the Midland), and heads north to start its journey south. It runs on Midland tracks all the way to Bristol, where it is handed over to the former Great Western Railway — in fact, before the war during the winter only a portion of it was worked through and most of the train never went near Devon at all. It is thus a continuation of a pattern of operation laid down in Edwardian times, which the reader may choose to take as an example of how backward and hidebound our railways are.

It is customary to disparage the whole creation of the LMSR and of British Railways as a process of taking-over by the Midland, but that was no bad thing for, in several ways, it was the most advanced company in Britain. It was the leader in passenger comfort, being the first to abolish the old third-class. It was the first to use centralised train control. It practised rigorous control of train loads, preferring a generality of moderately good services to a few crack trains and a lot of mediocre ones. Its stations were uniformly excellent, and wherever you went you would find the smallest structures all elegant, functional and unmistakably 'Midland'.

Technical Details

	Class 2MT	Class 3P	Class 5X	Class 5P5F	Hall class	5101' class
Overall length	38ft 9in	42ft	64ft 9in	63ft 8in	63ft	41ft
Weight: engine	63.5 tons	72.5 tons	79.5 tons	72 tons	75 tons	78.5 tons
tender	—	—	54.5 tons	54.5 tons	46.5 tons	—
Firegrate area	17.5sq ft	19sq ft	31sq ft	28.65sq ft	27.07sq ft	20.35sq ft
Heating surface	1,160sq ft	1,107sq ft	1,631sq ft	1,650sq ft	2,104sq ft	1,349sq ft
Boiler diameter	4ft 7in	4ft 9in	5ft 8.5in	5ft 8.5in	5ft 6in	5ft 0.5in
Boiler tube length	8ft 6in	10ft 10in	13ft 2.5in	13ft 2.5in	14ft 10in	11ft 0in
Boiler pressure	200lb/sq in	200lb/sq in	225lb/sq in	225lb/sq in	225lb/sq in	200lb/sq in
Cylinder bore	16in	17.5in	17in (three)	18.5in	18.5in	18in
Piston stroke	24in	26in	26in	28in	30in	30in
Coupled wheel dia.	5ft 0in	5ft 3in	6ft 9in	6ft 0in	6ft 0in	5ft.8in
Brakes	steam	steam	steam	steam	vacuum	steam
Coal capacity	3 tons	3 tons	9 tons	9 tons	6 tons	4 tons
Water capacity	1,350gal	1,500gal	4,000gal	4,000gal	4,000gal	2,000gal

Below:
The original '5X' class engine No 5552 as built with a domeless boiler and coupled to a standard tender of the 1930s. This engine later became No 45642 *Boscawen*.
Ian Allan Library

Overview

One reason we have not included a route map for this trip is the trite but true one that when working a train you have no control over where you go; another is that the railway network of the West Riding of Yorkshire is of staggering complexity and a description of it would be outside the scope of this book. The difficulty of locomotive working is largely determined by the gradients. The diagram shown is a simplified one; although the subtlest undulations of the road are significant when you have 60 unbraked wagons to control, they are less important for passenger train working. The heaviest work is clearly going to be over the gable south of Sheffield, where the line cuts through the eastern end of the Peak District. There is a long gradual ascent from the Trent valley through Birmingham to a summit in Warwickshire, where the abrupt drop is the Lickey Incline. By contrast, the Bristol & Exeter line across the Somerset moors is, apart from minor humps over bridges, the longest dead level line in the country, followed by the climb through the Blackdown Hills. The steepest gradients facing us are on the branch line between Newton Abbot and Torbay.

Part of our route was designed by George Stephenson. The North Midland Railway from Derby to Leeds was the last major railway project he worked on himself, and opened in the summer of 1840. It did not pass through Sheffield, which was on the end of a branch from Rotherham, but ran through the Rother valley to the east. It terminated in Leeds at what is now Hunslet Lane goods station, until in 1846 a connection was built to the new Leeds & Bradford Railway terminus at Wellington. The latter railway precipitated the downfall of George Hudson, the Railway King, for he persuaded the Midland Railway, formed in 1844 by amalgamation of the North Midland, Birmingham & Derby and Midland Counties Railways, to lease the Leeds & Bradford for a guaranteed 10% share dividend. When it leaked out that Hudson held most of those shares, the rest of his shady

deals were exposed and a domino collapse of railway finances followed.

The Birmingham & Derby line was another Stephenson project, built at the same period and running services from June 1839; its southern section from Whitacre to Lawley Street, now also a goods depot, opened in 1842. By then the Birmingham & Gloucester Railway was in business, a line which was originally surveyed by I. K. Brunel. However, the collision between narrow gauge and Brunel's broad gauge took place not in Birmingham but in Gloucester, with a terminus alongside that of the Bristol & Gloucester Railway. The latter, opened in 1844, was clearly destined to become part of the Great Western empire, but only a year later two of its directors were travelling to Paddington for a meeting and met on the train John Ellis, the Midland Deputy Chairman. Ellis offered them a more favourable lease on the spot, and by this chance the Midland reached Bristol.

The Bristol & Exeter Railway was effectively an extension of Brunel's Great Western, engineered by him and worked by the GW when it opened as far as Bridgwater in 1841. It was completed to Exeter in 1844, when there took place on 1 May that astonishing inaugural run to London in 4hr 44min. The progress of the rails farther west was somewhat slower; away from the centres of commerce, money was harder to find. Teignmouth was reached by 1846 and Newton Abbot at the close of that year. While this line, the South Devon Railway, was under construction, it proposed a branch from Aller to the port of Brixham, which was completed as far as Torquay in December 1848. An independent company, the Dartmouth & Torbay Railway, was formed later and constructed an extension to Paignton during 1858 and 1859. The final section into Kingswear, through difficult terrain and stretching local resources, was eventually opened on 10 August 1864.

Thus, it is not an excessive simplification to say that nearly the whole of this transport system, three hundred miles of state-of-the-art technology, was brought into being from nothing in about six years between 1836 and 1842. And this is only part of what was built then. Such an outpouring of energy knows no parallel whatever in human history. Nowadays it is customary to criticise the railways, but it is possible, to put it no stronger, that some of the perceived faults lie not in them but in a society which has not yet come to terms with the shake-up it was given by a small band of engineers a century ago.

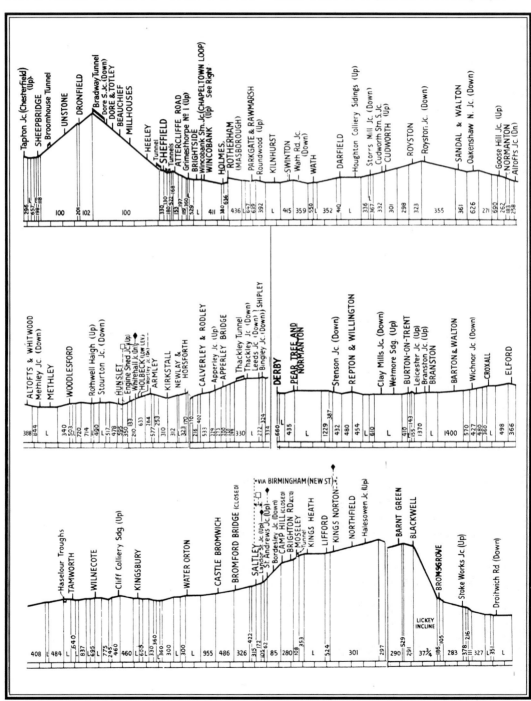

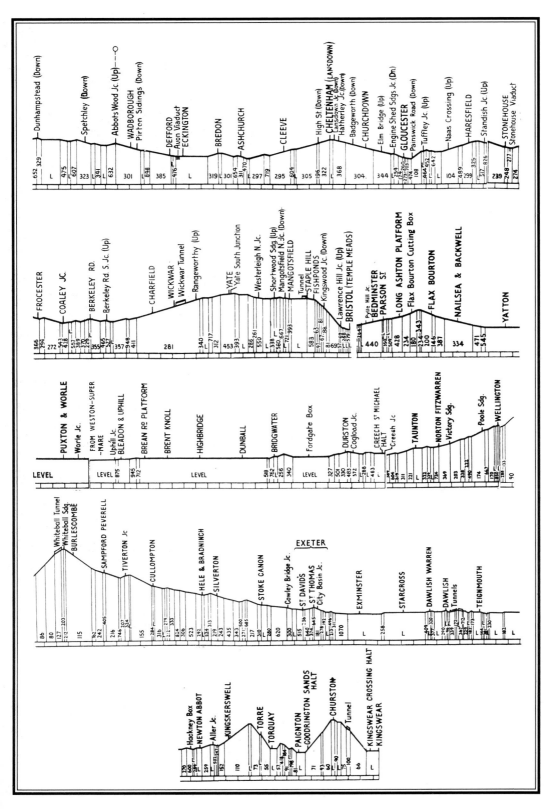

Machinery

The average speed of 41.6mph, excluding stops, quoted for the 'Devonian', may not strike you as all that fast for a crack express. There is a two-fold problem arising from the nature of the railway, serving the heart of a crowded and very busy country. Each of the 170 stations and depots from Bradford to Kingswear, and the 333 firms and public services that have private sidings on the route, need serving; at many of them a shunting goods train must occupy the main line and block it for 20min or so, and slow trains must be slotted in with fast ones. There is also traffic on and off other routes to fit in; our count of the number of junctions the train passes is 117. Many of the freight train and light engine movements cannot be rigidly scheduled but are arranged daily or hourly by Control according to the needs of the mines and factories. The route is operated by a total of 292 signalboxes. On this complex system, making any change to the train schedules is clearly an immense task, even without taking into account the difficulty of putting an acceleration into effect. The sheer amount of railway to be maintained puts a limit on the rate at which it can be upgraded to carry faster trains; there are curves which cannot practicably be removed; in the mining areas there is the constant menace of ground subsidence. The upshot of all this is that there are overall speed limits on the main lines of 65mph from Bradford to Leeds, 70mph to Cudworth, 60mph to Swinton Town Junction, 80mph to Hasland, 75mph to Ambergate, 85mph on the rest of the Midland route and 75mph west of Taunton. Only between Bristol and Cogload Junction is there no top speed limit.

One way for the Operating Department to raise train speeds is to ask the Locomotive Department for more engine power. In Midland days this was achieved by using two engines in place of one, and lately the London Midland Region has had to resort to the same expedient to attain not so much higher top speeds as quicker acceleration from the many stops and slows. The 'Devonian' is usually double-headed over the Midland line, on the climb to Whiteball Summit and over the steeply-graded Kingswear branch.

The locomotives most associated with this train are the 'Jubilees'. By the year 1932 the LMSR was sorely in need of more powerful, more modern engines in large numbers, and William A. Stanier, formerly

Below:
The re-equipment of the LMS in the 1930s brought a lot of work to contractors. This '5P5F' was built by Sir W. G. Armstrong Whitworth & Co of Newcastle and was painted in various shades of grey for the official works photograph. This also shows that Stanier engines at first carried a Great Western-style crosshead driven vacuum pump.
Sir W. G. Armstrong Whitworth & Co

Below:
In the evening of 17 May 1960, No 45699 *Galatea*, **possibly the best of the '5X' class engines, has arrived on Holbeck shed after working the down 'Devonian'. Fire-cleaning and ash-raking are in progress.** *G. W. Morrison*

the Great Western's Assistant Mechanical Engineer, was appointed to sort it out. He introduced an improved version of the GWR 'Hall' class 4-6-0 and also revamped some of the previous, basically Midland, designs with Swindon features such as the distinctive tapered boiler. The 4-6-0s came in two versions, the Class 5P5F with 6ft wheels and two cylinders and the Class 5XP with 6ft 9in wheels and three cylinders for express passenger work. (The '5' is a power rating.) They became known, from their liveries, as the 'Black' and 'Red' ones respectively; in 1935 '5XP' No 5642 was named *Silver Jubilee* and the others gradually acquired various martial and patriotic names, leading to the class becoming generally known as 'Jubilees'. The '5P5Fs' have always been called 'Black Fives' and are generally acknowledged to be the best general purpose steam locomotives ever built in Britain. They are rugged, straightforward to service, and will steam the better the harder they are pushed. After 20 years' work their frames are showing signs of strain and are being strengthened by welding in pieces of manganese-alloy steel in the highest-stressed areas around the axles, but that can hardly be counted a particular fault as all British engines are chronically weak in the main frames. The '5XPs' had a shaky beginning as their steaming was poor, with insufficient draught on the fire and inadequate cross-section through the superheater elements (which further heat the steam in its passage from the regulator valve to the cylinders). The boiler had to be redesigned, but they are now just as lively, reliable and vice-free as the others. The extra cylinder, though an additional expense, makes them smoother as they have six piston strokes instead of four to each wheel revolution, and gives them the edge for fast running. There are 191 '5XPs', and the '5P5Fs', including the similar British Railways derivative, will finally total 1,014 engines.

South of Bristol the train is hauled by an ex-GWR 4-6-0, a 'Hall' or the four-cylinder version, a 'Castle'. These originated in the intensive development effort at Swindon around the turn of the century, which culminated in No 98, the prototype of all the medium-sized 4-6-0s that have been built ever since. A total of 547 engines were built to the same basic design with very little change over 47 years, although even the staunchest Great Western fan should

concede that some improvements could have been made in that time. The Stanier Class 5s, for example, have more modern injectors and more accessible valve motion.

Between Bradford and Leeds the motive power is provided by a tank engine. This sounds like another instance of the way Bradford has been treated as a mere satellite of Leeds, but consider a moment. A tender is an appreciable addition to the load the engine has to pull, and the only reason it is there is because a boiler capable of sustained high power becomes too large to leave enough room for sufficient fuel to be carried. Where distances are short and there is no need for a long operating range between visits to the depot for coal and water, a tender is not needed and the weight of fuel will be useful on the engine to aid in adhesion. When the high-speed 'West Riding' train was introduced in 1937 a pair of 'N2' class 0-6-2Ts was judged better to haul it between Leeds and Bradford than the latest 'A4' streamliners. Most passenger trains on the ex-LMS routes are hauled by 2-6-4Ts or 2-6-2Ts. The Lancashire & Yorkshire Railway used 2-4-2Ts with complete success on express trains, and so highly regarded were they that recently, notwithstanding the plenitude of more modern types, three of them, Nos 50636, 50686 and 50795, were transferred to Bradford Manningham depot for the top passenger turns. On today's run, however, we are rostered one of the taper boiler 2-6-2Ts. These were part of the Stanier programme and were considered by the staff to be inferior to the previous Derby version, which itself had a guaranteed non-steaming boiler and valves and cylinders designed for sluggish performance. It is standard practice for enginemen to dismiss new engine types as worse than those they replace, but in this case there was truth in the opinion, and from 1941 new boilers were built for these engines; larger and with nearly twice the superheater capacity. At least they have decent long-travel valves which give the steam a chance of actually propelling the engine.

Turning now to the human side of the system, both the engine and the crew for the first leg come from Manningham. It is a small depot, with about 30 engines: 2-6-2Ts and 2-6-4Ts, some of the ubiquitous standard 0-6-0Ts for shunting and a couple of Midland Compounds used on turns to

Morecambe. The building is a Midland roundhouse built in stone in 1868 and apparently untouched since.

The Leeds-Bristol run is normally worked throughout by engines and crews from the Midland depot at Bristol (Barrow Road). The 206 miles take 5.5hr, to which is added the time taken for booking on and off and running between station and depot at each end, making a heavy day's work. It is indeed the top job at Bristol and the only lodging turn. It employs two sets of men, or four if the train is double-headed, who work north one day, stay overnight in Leeds and return the next day. There is a love-hate relationship between enginemen and lodging turns; as pay is linked to a combination of time on duty and distance worked, with an additional allowance for lodging, the money is popular, but no one would prefer inner-city digs or the staff hostel to one's own home. Their engine is serviced at Leeds Holbeck depot, and woe betide the mechanical staff there if anything happens to it before the return journey.

The Bristol-Paignton leg is the return working of an engine and crew from Newton Abbot. The engine will probably be remanned at Newton, for although the run down the branch is a short one, in the event of traffic delays the process of getting down there and back to the shed can be protracted. It is highly desirable to arrange matters so that not only are men not forced to work excessive hours but also they do not finish too late to be able to take up their next turn of duty.

That is what is supposed to happen: but a railway is not a clockwork mechanism, it is a collection of human beings serving a human community. On the day we have chosen to travel there are some expected and unexpected variations.

A special party has booked from Bradford to Bristol, and they are to be accommodated in two extra coaches attached to the 'Devonian'. This will take the load over what is allowed for one engine, which is no problem between Leeds and Bristol, but a second engine must be found from Bradford, while the Western Region are asked to decide whether the extra coaches are to go through, in which case they also may have to allocate additional engines. At Manningham the problem is solved by borrowing one of the new Ivatt 2-6-2Ts whose principal jobs are local passenger services

such as the push-pulls to Keighley.

Yesterday afternoon a driver and fireman who were expecting to spend the day on preparation and disposal duties, relieving on shunting engines or just waiting in case someone else fails to turn up, received an instruction to book on at 7.55am, prepare a Class 2MT tank engine and work to orders. There are some assumptions underlying that bald statement: that the orders exist and have been given to those who have to implement them; that the engine is available and is a type permitted to go where the orders specify; that the men have signed for the route, that is, they are conversant with it; that the extra coaches are available and there will be a shunter ready who knows which ones they are and where they are; and so on. All the details have to be tackled by someone. Then information and instructions must pass between the various offices and out to the drivers, firemen, fitters, shunters, carriage examiners, guards and labourers who will do the repairs, oil the axles, light the fires, fill the tanks, replenish the lavatory paper, clean the windows, change the points and finally move the train.

The above was worked out in advance and is the easy part. The tricky part is that, also yesterday, the booked engines never got to Leeds at all. A problem with the vacuum brake equipment arose and, by arrangement between the Birmingham, Derby and Leeds Control Rooms, they were taken off at an out-of-course stop at Burton. (In this context, railway fiction often gives the impression that in the rare event of an engine breaking down on the road, the crew are treated as having broken down with it. In practice, when a substitute is provided they will take it over and finish the job.) Holbeck depot has to produce something to power the southbound train, and word has been put through what are best described as alternative channels of communication that it had better be good. The Bristol men have been mollified by assurances that their own mounts should be ready to take up the working again at Birmingham.

That the railway is a cumbersome machine is undeniable. That trains do not just happen to run should be clear. That all this work is done on the 'Devonian' and countless other trains, under the relentless invigilation of the clock, day after day, is the achievement of the men who are the machine.

Above:
The tools of the trade. Bucket, firing shovel, hand-brush and coal-pick, and the handles of fire-irons poking out from their stowage rack.

Photographed on the 'Hall' class engine *Burton Agnes Hall*, at the Great Western Society's Didcot Railway Centre.
C. J. Austin

Bradford to Leeds

Since it is statistically likely that the majority of readers come from what they consider more comfortable parts of the country, they may subscribe to the stock image of northern industrial towns as harsh, dirty and caring for nowt but 'brass'. It is certainly true that industry is prominent, but in the 20th century it does at least wear a human face, even if it is often a dour one. At the feet of the huge square blocks of the mills may be found surfaces of untamed rock, while behind their roofs rise green hills. The towns have not forgotten the fast streams and upland pastures that brought them their wealth.

The heights of Baildon Moor are visible from the platforms of Bradford Forster Square station, named after W. E. Forster, Member of Parliament for Bradford in 1870 and founder of our national education system. Around it are civic buildings as well-proportioned as you may find in any spa town. Three hundred yards to the south is the other station, Exchange. To have two termini separated by such a gap is of course utterly ludicrous, especially as there is no barrier in the gap except buildings. True, to close it would require extensive reconstruction in the city centre, but the local disruption would be far outweighed by the benefit to the town as a whole. When the stations were built by the Leeds & Bradford and Lancashire & Yorkshire Railways respectively, those were private companies and had no powers to force a connection through. However, under the British Transport Commission we may expect it to be a top priority.

The basis of Bradford's relegation to the end of a branch line is geographical: the line takes what in the 1840s was seen as the only practical route, down the Bradford Beck to join the Aire Valley at Shipley. This defile is so narrow that at the Bradford end the entire area that is naturally level is filled up by the railway. The station was built in 1846 on what is now the eastern side of the goods sidings, rebuilt by the Midland in 1890 when it was one of the first to have electric lighting, rebuilt by the LMS in 1932 and refurbished in 1953 when its overall roof was replaced by pre-fab platform awnings. The façade and the adjoining Midland Hotel are original parts of the 1890 station. Beside it is a large shed, Valley goods station, and north of School Street bridge a broad fan of rolling stock sidings. Beyond that is another goods station, Trafalgar Street, then immediately beyond the end of its shunting neck is Manningham station. Here the four running lines, west and east departure and west and east arrival, become two and are joined by two independent goods lines, and the shed lies on the east side of the station. This area is dominated by the great Manningham Mills, opened in 1873 and owned by Samuel Cunliffe Lister, whose munificence is commemorated by nearby Lister Park.

In the permanent gloaming of the roundhouse we find our allocated engines. The Class 3 tank is No 40114, one of eight based here. She was built at Derby, completed on 3 August 1935, and, as discussed earlier, subsequently rebuilt with Class 6A boiler No 9952. She was last overhauled at Horwich last March. In another stall is Class 2MT No 41247. This one was built at Crewe, although allocated to Derby running shed from issue on 24 October 1949 until sent to Manningham on loan on 23 May 1953. The loan proved successful and five of the class were transferred to the shed on 10 April 1954. No 41247 was overhauled at Crewe last November, so we should have quite a smooth ride. These engines are in great demand; they are economical, good runners, and even more important, convenient to prepare, dispose and carry out routine servicing. Compared with the old Midland 0-6-0s, being rostered one of these is as good as a holiday.

There is no one about No 41247, as the driver has inspected the moving parts and filled the oil reservoirs on the motion, and has gone to make a brew of tea, while the fireman has checked that the smokebox

17

Above:
Manningham engine shed. The notice reads: 'Midland Railway notice to drivers, firemen and all concerned. STOP. All engines requiring to enter the shed must be brought to a stand at this board. By Order.' The fireman of 2-6-0 No 43044 is waiting while his mate backs her in. *J. S. Hancock*

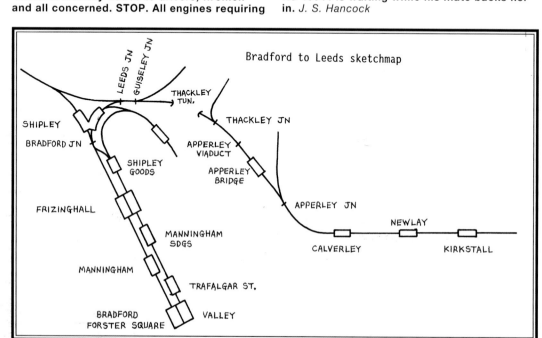

Bradford to Leeds sketchmap

LEEDS JN
GUISELEY JN
THACKLEY TUN.
THACKLEY JN
SHIPLEY
BRADFORD JN
APPERLEY VIADUCT
SHIPLEY GOODS
APPERLEY BRIDGE
FRIZINGHALL
APPERLEY JN
NEWLAY
MANNINGHAM SDGS
CALVERLEY
KIRKSTALL
MANNINGHAM
TRAFALGAR ST.
BRADFORD FORSTER SQUARE
VALLEY

and ashpan are empty and sandboxes full, made up the fire with some lumps thrown on by hand, and gone to the stores. By the time he returns with the lamps, flags, detonators and spanners which must be carried on all engines, plus a shovel — if there was one on board, someone pinched it during the night — the fire has burnt up and steam pressure is rising. He turns the blower on and busies himself cleaning the cab windows, washing down the floor, and taking off and cleaning the boiler water gauge protectors, taking care to shut off and drain the gauges first. When the driver returns pressure is up to 150lb, enabling them to test the injectors, sanders and brakes. Then he closes the ashpan dampers, shuts the blower off and leaves the sliding firedoors just ajar, so that he will not cause a nuisance by making smoke or blowing-off while they are shunting.

A task for the fireman is to position the turntable in line with our stall, warn the men who are working on an engine opposite, and beckon the driver forward. A roar of steam from No 41247's cylinder drain cocks fills the shed, then dies away as she moves, followed by five bonks as she inches on to the turntable, leaving the condensate from her cocks to join the oily puddles on the shed floor. When she is turned to face away from the shed entrance, the fireman again goes ahead to warn anyone about the door before signalling the driver to follow him out. In the yard they top up the water tanks, then at nine o'clock the driver calls up the signalman from a telephone by the shed exit signal, to tell him which duty we are. The signal comes off and we pull out on to the main line, running bunker-first, towards the city.

One shortcoming of Forster Square is that the carriage cleaning sidings on the west side are on the short side, so the 'Devonian' set is split between two of them. After stopping at the box to pick up a shunter, we cross to the west departure line, reunite the train and push it into Platform 3, because although the 11 coaches fit comfortably in any platform except 1, this is the only road which can accept the extended train without fouling any points. Next we run into Platform 6 and shunt forward into the sidings. There we collect the extra two coaches, put them on the east arrival line and run round them via the adjoining engine line. The signalman does not like us to run up the arrival line, so we push back into the platform,

draw forward over the crossovers and set back on to the train. These movements take some time, as the signalman has other traffic to deal with at the same time: the 9.32am all-stations to Leeds is being put into Platform 2, a push-pull worked by one of No 41247's sisters leaves for Skipton at 9.15am, and five minutes later the 8.46am from Ilkley runs in. Also, coupling up passenger coaches is not simple. When the shunter has brought the vehicles together and is satisfied that they are not going to move, he ducks in between and takes both vacuum hoses off their dummies. He takes one of the screw couplings and checks that the screw is centrally disposed between its two loops, lifts it on to the opposite drawhook and screws it up until, with the buffers touching, it has no slack. The handle is left with the ball downwards and its hinged top dropped into a locating lug. Then he couples up the lighting control cables, steam heat pipes if train heating is wanted, and vacuum hoses. The flexible gangway bellows are pulled together and latched. All these components are big and heavy, dirty and often cold and wet. Lastly he must climb into all guards' compartments and release the handbrakes before ordering the engine driver to move off.

It is nearly 9.30am when we are in position and No 40114 appears and is coupled on in front. The train now comprises 13 coaches, with seats for 468 passengers plus the restaurant crew and guard, 817ft in length and weighing about 445 tons, excluding the length and weight of the engines.

On the LMR coupling up is an Operating Department job, but our driver walks back to see that it has been done properly. Working the brake will be the responsibility of the leading engine, and he is heard to remark that it will probably use all the steam the latter can produce. No 41247 has done the shunting with no addition to her fire, but now our fireman builds it up, a little at a time with the blower on to avoid smoke, until he has a good box-full, albeit with pressure still only at 160lb. The guard comes up to add particulars of the engines to his journal, then in our cab we can watch the vacuum gauge needle rise, fall sharply, rise again and fall slowly as the brakes are tested. No 40114's fireman places lamps in Class A position over the buffers and, as we judge from the display of smoke, goes to worry at his fire.

The arrival of the 8.40am train from Hellifield is our sign to board the footplate and check round; the signals are already off, for the east departure line, as the signalman has also to accept the 7.50am from Sheffield and the 9.26am from Ilkley in quick succession. We are standing ahead of the platform starter, so after the guard has broken out his green flag the station inspector comes down to give us verbal permission from the signalbox to start, acknowledged by both drivers. On time at 9.50am, both men open their regulators slightly and ease the big train into motion.

For the first few turns we can see nothing, surrounded by steam from two lots of cylinder cocks, but when they are closed the fog clears in time for us to exchange waves with the fireman on the passing Sheffield train. The start is unspectacular and fairly slow: there are speed limits of 10mph in the station area and 20mph through Manningham. We put No 41247 into 30% cut-off and half regulator, and leave her there. Past Frizinghall (whose signalbox is destined in future years to move into the next valley and signal Oakworth) speed rises, so both regulators are eased with a view to stopping at Shipley. No 40114 immediately starts blowing off, which shows the unwisdom of

overdoing it when you have only 14 miles to go, and that all downhill. Still, it gives a good show as we coast into the sharply curved platform; we stop well forward with our two extra coaches off the end. All signals are still on, for the Ilkley train is late coming across Guiseley Junction, but it runs past during our halt. The full traction available from the pair of engines is now needed for the restart and the haul out of the bend on to the main line with both engines barking their loudest. That is actually the only hard pulling on this leg, and it is not necessary to put any more coal on the fire, so really there is nothing else to report from the footplate of No 41247. The only thing we have to do is watch the road, as although the braking is done by the man in front that does not relieve us of the responsibility of observing the signals and acting if necessary.

From Shipley Leeds Junction we are on the slow line, not implying that this is a slow train but because the lines from Keighley and the north come alongside on our left and are called the fast lines. In fact, we are overhauling the 9.32am stopper, which has crossed to the fast line and is due into Leeds at the same time as we are. The fast lines were added as late as 1901, needing a new tunnel alongside the

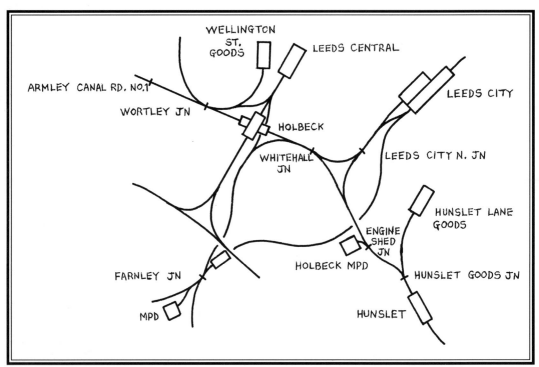

Above:
This view of Manningham was taken after closure, but it shows the complete installation: the station on the left; a train on the down passenger line; beyond the little down side waiting shelter, the shed offices and water tank, kept warm by the sand drying furnace beneath; the shed entrance, ashpit and coal road; and the solidly-built coal store.
C. T. Gifford

original bore, 1,518yd long, of Thackley tunnel, the biggest engineering work on the line. Emerging from this, we cross the first of several bridges over the Leeds & Liverpool Canal and the River Aire, pass the branch to Esholt sewage works and cruise down a valley pleasantly rural until the factories of Leeds crowd about us. Whitaker & Ackroyd and the Kirkstall Forge have sidings here. The ruined church on the left is 12th century Kirkstall Abbey. Between Kirkstall and Armley Canal Road the slow lines climb over a flyover to land on the north side of the other two. However, here again the addition to our load has caused complications, since the train is too long to fit in the terminal platforms at Leeds Wellington. Therefore it is switched to another pair of metals which do not go over the flyover but debouch into the fast lines beneath it. The 9.32am is meanwhile turned slow line at Armley Canal Road No 1. We are thus still on the south side of the formation, and the Leeds City diagram shows how this enables us to enter the through platforms of Leeds New. We continue past Wortley Junction, where the Harrogate line heads off north, past the connection from the Calder valley at Whitehall Junction, and round a long curve

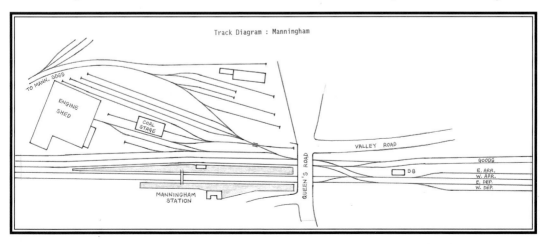

past the Government-owned Monk Bridge Iron Works to Leeds City North Junction.

Although combined under the title of Leeds City since 1938, the two stations are still operationally almost separate; Wellington is the original Leeds & Bradford terminus, shared by the North Midland's extension from its terminus at Hunslet Lane south of the river, and New is a joint London & North Western and North Eastern station opened in 1869. The latter is built on brick arches straddling the river at the entrance to the canal. With the Great Northern and Lancashire & Yorkshire station, Leeds Central, nearby, we have here the pivotal point in transport for the eastern half of England. It is a result of the way the old companies each developed their own facilities that all through passenger trains have to reverse here, although that is no great hardship as every train is going to stop in the principal city of the north. Leeds, a farming village at the time of the Normans, owed its rise to the woollen and clothing trades and later diversified into heavy engineering. The district of Hunslet is of special interest to us as it is one of the world centres of locomotive manufacture. Matthew Murray's Round Foundry, builders of the first portable steam engines; Fenton, Murray & Jackson; Kitson's; Wilson's; Manning, Wardle; Hudswell, Clarke; John Fowler the road locomotive builders; the Hunslet Engine Co; household names in the world of railways. Also in Hunslet, the Tetley brewery doubtless helps sustain the output of the factories.

Left:
Inside the shed, 2-6-4T No 42189 on the central turntable being made ready to go out. Both she and No 42152 in the background are blowing-off, but at the late date of 13 February 1967, that probably just means the safety valves are scored and leaky.
J. H. Cooper-Smith

Above right:
Our Stanier 2-6-2T, No 40114, seen hauling an up express from Bradford eastwards out of Shipley. Behind her are the fast lines; to the left is the Great Northern branch line from Laisterdyke.
K. Field

Below right:
A driver's-eye view before you board the 2-6-2T, No 40202 on Birkenhead shed. Through the side window can be seen the reverser handle, and the position of the radius rod at the bottom of the expansion link shows that the engine has been left in full forward gear.
K. Hughes

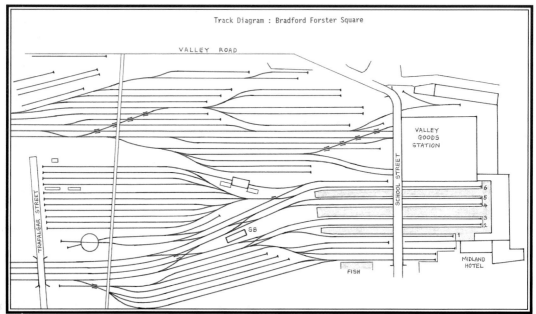

Track Diagram : Bradford Forster Square

Above left:
Our Class 2 2-6-2T No 41247.
This was taken when she
was based at Derby, and is
here doing the station north
shunt. *E. Treacy*

Above:
**A view towards Bradford
Forster Square station from
the long footbridge. A diesel
train is pulling out on the
east departure line while a
filthy 2-6-4T is on the west
arrival line heading for
Platform 6. In the middle distance are the carriage repair
shed and signalbox, and in
the background the square
mass of Valley goods station.**
G. W. Morrison

Centre right:
**At the inner end of Forster
Square platforms, the cheap
and nasty BR awnings and a
couple of worn-out 2-6-4Ts,
and a guard has a word with
a porter on 22 April 1966.**
H. A. Gamble

Below right:
**Bradford Forster Square: the
Midland Hotel pictured on
7 October 1993.** *SHA*

Left:
With a full head of steam and a big fire, one of the last '5Xs' in service, No 45697 *Achilles,* **departs with the Bradford-Heysham parcels on 29 April 1967.**
G. W. Morrison

Below left:
No 42085, dirty but quite able to deal with the 10 coaches of a London express, comes into Shipley on 21 March 1967. Shipley Goods signal-box is by the rear of the train and the wagons are in Shipley Town sidings. This engine survived to be pre-served and is now based on the Lakeside & Haverthwaite Railway. *G. W. Morrison*

Above right:
2-6-2T No 40117 standing on the release road opposite Forster Square signalbox with a train she has brought in from Shipley, in May 1956.
P. Ransome-Wallis

Centre right:
The west end of Thackley tunnel, viewed from a bridge which is still there, although the neat little shed unfortu-nately is not. On the down fast is the 9am St Pancras-Edinburgh express of 7 May 1955; the locomotive is No 46109 *Royal Engineer.*
C. W. Bendall

Below right:
Another spring scene west of Leeds; the train is the up 'Thames-Clyde Express', hauled by '5P5F' No 45082 and 'Royal Scot' No 46113 *Cameronian.* **The train is caught crossing the river by Whittaker & Ackroyd's at Newlay. Adjoining the bridge are electric repeaters for the Newlay home signals.**
A. M. Ross

Above:
Looking the other way from the previous view, Newlay & Horsforth station was photographed on 11 May 1961, with the through train from Bristol passing on the down slow, hauled with ease by 2-6-4T No 42139.
G. W. Morrison

Left:
On the approaches to Leeds at Wortley Junction: ahead is the bridge carrying the Great Northern line into Leeds Central, and the tracks curving up to the left go to Wellington Street goods. The cheerless platform of Holbeck Low Level, a winner of a Worst Station contest, is visible at the far end of the Bristol-Bradford train, on 9 March 1961 with 11 on but still hauled by a single 2-6-4T. The chimney in the background is part of the Tetley brewery. *G.W. Morrison*

Above:
'Jubilee' No 45608 *Gibraltar* lifts the up 'Devonian' from Leeds City Platform 5. Behind the train is the Queen's Hotel, and on the left Whitehall Road power station. *K. Field*

Right:
No 41255 has brought a train up from Bradford and is now standing at the west end of Platform 9 at Leeds City station on 6 October 1951. Prominent on the smokebox door is the shed plate '25C' — Goole — and 'SC' — self-cleaning — meaning the smokebox contains baffle plates which are claimed to prevent ash from settling inside. *K. Field*

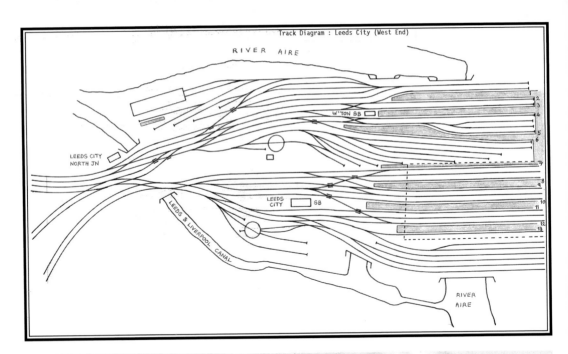

Track Diagram : Leeds City (West End)

RIVER AIRE

LEEDS CITY
NORTH JN

W'TON SB

LEEDS
CITY   SB

LEEDS & LIVERPOOL CANAL

RIVER
AIRE

Leeds to Birmingham

Holbeck locomotive depot is a standard Midland roundhouse type with two turntables. Outside, each approach road passes beneath a coaling plant of the type which lifts wagons and tips their contents into an overhead hopper, and over an ash pit with a mechanical ash loading plant in which the ash is shovelled into tubs which are tipped into wagons. Engines going off shed run round the outsides of the pit roads. There are storage sidings on the north side of the yard, and a repair shop on the south.

At about the time the 'Devonian' is being readied in Bradford, the Bristol men are entering the office off Nineveh Road to see what awaits them. It has been noted that Holbeck are expected to provide some decent motive power, and on booking on we find that they have turned out one of their best and most famous engines: '5X' No 45562 *Alberta*. She was built by the North British Locomotive Co in Glasgow and delivered in August 1934; as one of the early batch she has since been rebuilt with the redesigned boiler. She was last overhauled in May 1956 at Crewe Works, when it is noted she was assembled with boiler No 8626, coupled to tender No 9774, and given manganese liners to the coupled axleboxes — expensive but highly wear-resistant. She went to Derby Works for a Light Casual repair in March, so we have an engine that is pretty well on the top line. Our colleagues are not quite so well served, as they have been given a '5P5F', No 45407. They anticipate a less comfortable ride.

After signing on and reading the notices, we collect the engine and get off shed.

Left:
A view over the west end of Leeds City, showing the separation of the stations, New on the left and Wellington on the right. In the distance a diesel train is coming past City North Junction signalbox. There the canal and river curve right and the railway goes round to the left of the big pale roofs, which are the Monk Bridge Iron Works, to Wortley where the gasholder is. *Ian Allan Library*

One consolation is that the fireman has his personal shovel with him, and this he uses with determination. He is taking no chances with this foreigner. As the engines back down towards City the blowers are on and layers of coal are being added to build up a mass of fire almost up to the firehole rim. The vacuum brake is coupled up and strictly should be used, but at present neither engine has her brake ejector on and the drivers are using the short run to try the responses of the engine brakes individually. Stanier engines have steam brakes on both engine and tender, and making several applications serves to warm up the cylinders. When the vacuum is in use the steam brake valve is actuated by a vacuum-operated piston, and the connecting lever may be worked by hand to apply the steam brake independently. The live steam injector (a Gresham & Craven 11mm) is used in bursts to keep pressure down, gradually filling the boiler.

On arrival at City we run into the centre road between Platforms 11 and 12, to contemplate the gloom inside the three arches of the overall roof. We have a good tenderful of coal, well damped down, and while waiting we hose down the floor and wipe round the cab interior with a bit of cotton waste to complete a smart turnout. The two tank engines wheel in the train well up to time at 10.12am.

As soon as the ground signal in front of us shows a white light we move out (creating vacuum this time) and No 45407's driver, behind us, drops us back on the train. He then shuts off his brake ejector, releases the vacuum from train pipe and chamber and puts his brake handle in the 'OFF' position. The guard comes to give us the load, and a shunter, who has uncoupled the engines from the other end, arrives to couple us on. We create vacuum with *Alberta's* large ejector and make a test application from each engine in turn to check that the steam brakes operate.

We do not know whether any of the passengers carry maps and are aware that half an hour after leaving Bradford they are

Left:
No 41265, a Manningham engine, leaving the Wellington side of Leeds City and about to turn left to Hunslet, on a local to Normanton on 18 November 1953. *K. Field*

Left:
View north from Nineveh Road at Engine Shed Junction, showing Holbeck Loco. A long train of empties hauled by a Class 8F 2-8-0 has come round the Whitehall curve and is taking to the slow line.
Ian Allan Library

Left:
The view from the coaling tower at Holbeck, with the twin ash loading plants. The engine on the left is probably having its smokebox emptied, since the blower is on. To the right of the diesel a fireman is filling his tank; on the far right three engines are parked ready for duty. The date is 13 April 1966.
L. A. Nixon

still exactly the same distance from Torbay, or perhaps they are just resigned to it. Anyhow, now the journey proper starts. When the station staff are ready to send us off we have to give two long and one 'crow' hoots on the whistle as a request to the box for the road south. Given the right-away and a hand acknowledgement from behind, we put her in full forward gear, sound the whistle and open the regulator by about one third. The LMS regulator valve is a slide valve working over ports on the top of the steam supply pipe inside the dome on the boiler. Over it is another valve which opens smaller ports, and this first valve is opened by the initial movement of the regulator handle. The main valve is worked by a pin moving in a slot and only begins to move after the first valve is open. This gives better control over the steam supply when starting the engine, but once the main valve is open the handle has to be brought back some way, shutting the first valve, before it begins to close, so it does not lend itself to fine adjustment. It is best used by keeping on first valve at low speeds, then opening up full when we are well under way and controlling the engine thereafter by the reverser. So, on full first valve we take her away.

A '5X' starting a heavy load is the most stupendous thrill to all the senses that ever art or artifice devised. The exhaust blast is a woof through the firehole and a series of whumps off the chimney, throwing out a good deal of smoke from that huge fire. As we get going and open on to main valve her voice rises to a full-bodied roar, sheer irresistible force expressed in sound, a shout of unleashed energy which knows no true imitation. Mingling with the slower, deeper beat from No 45407 behind, every stroke of Alberta's three pistons is cried to the town. It may be fanciful to compare the thrust of the rods to the thud of horses' hooves writ vast, but it certainly laughs to scorn the fretful buzz of internal-combustion engines or the dreary whine of electric machines.

As we pass Engine Shed Junction our driver starts to wind the reverser handle back, as the speed limit is 30mph here and 40mph at Hunslet Goods Junction. With the train under way, we can look out for an overbridge near Hunslet station and a branch line and yard on the down side at Hunslet South Junction. This is the Middleton Railway. Wagonways were introduced to this area by colliery owner Charles Brandling of Killingworth in about 1750, and to connect his mines to Leeds

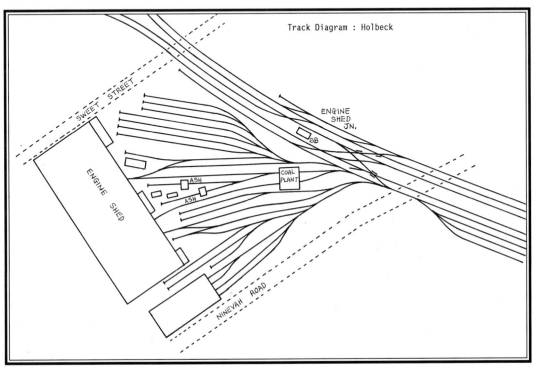

Track Diagram : Holbeck

SWEET STREET

ENGINE SHED JN.

SB

COAL PLANT

ENGINE SHED

ASH

ASH

NINEVAH ROAD

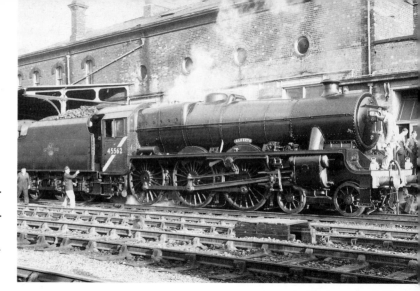

Left:
Walking into the grime and gloom of Holbeck shed, you find your engine. *R. Lush*

Above right:
A portrait of our '5X', No 45562 *Alberta*. This was taken in October 1967, when she was kept very smart by the staff for special trips. The yellow stripe on the cab side is a recent device meaning that the engine is not to run beneath the electric traction wires south of Crewe. The cylinder in front of the cab is a vacuum reservoir for the Automatic Warning System, whose receiver can be seen under the front. The fireman checks that his smokebox door is tight. *J. W. Ellson*

Below right:
Topside detail on '5X' No 45675 *Hardy*. Two Ross safety valves, steam dome cover, and boiler feed clack valve cover. The feed pipes are concealed in the boiler lagging. This was taken at Carnforth on 17 June 1967 and the engine was to work the 9.55am parcels to Leeds. *Alberta* was on the 10.55am to Bradford. *P. Claxton*

he formed the first railway company to be established by an Act of Parliament on 9 June 1758. The railway changed over to steam haulage for all traffic on 12 August 1812. This was the first use of powered land transport anywhere in the world, and its consequences have been so profound that it is really quite impossible to overestimate the importance of Middleton or of that date in human history. It seems quite astonishing to the writer that people who claim to be educated, and can give chapter and verse on all sorts of poets and painters, are ignorant of the date and place that shaped the way we live and our view of the world. Still, they may prefer to muse on the romance of the past amid Kirkstall's peace than to consider the smoking factories, the winding towers at Rothwell and Waterloo, the vast marshalling yard at Stourton and the tainted water of the Aire & Calder Navigation.

The Stanier firehole has a flap, hinged at the bottom, which may be flipped up to cover about a third of the hole. The gap between it and the baffle plate which protrudes into the box above the hole is just enough to get the shovel in without admitting too much air. Although *Alberta's* safety valves are lifting, the fireman sets to work with the shovel, building up the back of the fire until the flap is needed to keep it in. He opens the front damper full and starts the exhaust steam injector, a Davies & Metcalfe 11mm. On this type the water valve and live/exhaust steam shuttle valve are automatic, so it is only necessary to check that the water tap on the tender is open, turn on the steam and adjust the feed rate with the water control handle by his seat. The regulator is now wide open and the thunder from the chimney is merging with the general rumble at speed. A stranger might begin to think that the engine has no springs, but that is because with such a great weight to carry the spring rates are very high, and they translate every irregularity in the rail to the floor on which we are standing. The heat from the fire becomes ferocious. The intimacy between man and machine so dwelt upon by advocates of the steam engine now explains itself, for if you did not feel yourself in profound sympathy with this scorching, draughty, ear-shattering, bone-shaking conveyance you would not stand it for five minutes, let alone five hours.

At Methley North Junction we get a distant 'on' and have to slow down until we see that the Intermediate Block signal at Altofts station has cleared, but in any case we have to keep to 25mph through Altofts Junction and 15mph to negotiate the curves at Normanton. The reason for the check was a train of mineral empties, due out of Hunslet Sidings at 9.40am and past Altofts at 10.30am, and running slightly late. We overtake it on the slow line at Goose Hill Junction. The short section between these two junctions was of immense importance in the early years, as it was where the lines from Manchester, York, Leeds and Derby met, and all north-south traffic came this way. Normanton was thus a key station, and its imposing buildings and huge platform remind us of the days when it was the refreshment stop for the Scottish expresses.

From here we leave the Calder valley, and from the slow start the slight, but significant, up-grade is a hard slog. Through Normanton both engines are blowing-off deafeningly, but that ceases as they get stuck into it. The fireman is soon walloping more coal into the box, his accuracy undeterred by the engine's attempts to throw him off balance. The last few shovelfuls of each round he puts on the back, nearly blocking the opening. The sliding doors he leaves open. The pressure gauge needle stays fixed near the red line.

Hard pounding continues until we are over the top at Royston and speed reaches a mile a minute for the first time. The riding is decidedly lively, for which you should blame the Coal Board's excavations: St Johns, Sharlston, Walton, Monckton Main, Carlton Main, Ferrymoor; those are just the nearest where the ground under us is turned inside-out, a Hunslet-built tank engine shunts among black heaps and a BR engine, nearly always an 'eight' 2-8-0, dirt-black, pulls away another load of black coal.

Most of the goods and shunting engines work to Control orders, but there is a plethora of timetabled goods workings around us. The 9.35am Bradley Wood-Staveley Ironworks freight is waiting for a path at Royston Junction. An engine which has just lifted the coal empties from Royston locomotive depot is augmenting that load in Carlton Main Sidings for an 11.15am departure. A light engine, 10.5am off Royston, is standing at Storrs Mill Junction waiting to continue southwards. Between Royston and Rotherham we pass no fewer than eight down workings in

Above:
Preparing for the road: No 45668 *Madden* is oiled at Willesden shed on 30 April 1955.
G. Clarke

Below:
A non-resident Class 5P5F is seen at Holbeck: No 45335 of Kentish Town.
T. Booth

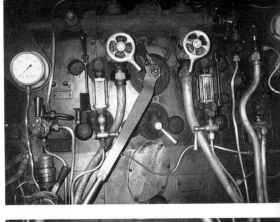

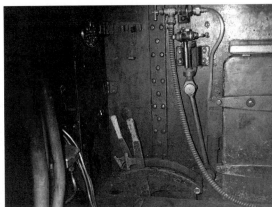

Above:
The driver's controls on a '5X'. This is the preserved No 5593 *Kolhapur*, which has the latest additions of a speedometer and AWS. The isolating cock for turning on the system lies to the left of the reverser handle and the valve for applying the brake lies to its right. Uncomfortably close to the driver are three steam pipes carrying steam to two vacuum ejectors and the engine steam brake. The reverser has a latch which you release by turning the nearer hand grip inwards. The oil box below forms a nice footrest. *SHA*

Below:
The shovelling plate on a Stanier tender is a crude affair, with an afterthought of a barrier to stop too much coal falling out. On either side of it are water supply valve handles; above it is a pair of opening doors. *SHA*

Above left:
Boiler backhead on a '5X' class engine. On the left is the train-pipe vacuum gauge marked in inches of mercury, on the right the boiler pressure gauge marked in pounds per square inch. The engine is not in steam, but is ready to light up; the gauge-glasses do not show up well, but the water level is just below halfway. After dark the only illumination in the cab is a small paraffin lamp, placed on a bracket to the left of the left-hand gauge-glass. These foot-plate views were taken at Loughborough by kind permission of the Great Central Railway. *SHA*

Left:
Firehole on a '5X', with doors open and flap up. Across the top is a hinged plate intended to shield the firelight from the driver's eyes. The adjoining pipes have taken countless blows from fire-irons and clinker shovels over the years. *SHA*

Lower left:
Fireman's side of the cab; hose-pipe and tap, exhaust injector water control, two damper handles sprouting from the floor. To the right is the seat with AWS battery box beneath it. *SHA*

Bottom left:
The controls on '5P5F' No 5231 are less cluttered because she has no AWS, so this is more of a mid-1950s cab; however, the vacuum gauge is BR. (For those readers who know the *Ballad of John Axon*, it was the joint below the large ejector handle that failed, sending a jet of steam out towards the camera and denying him access to regulator, brake and reverser.) *SHA*

Right:
Tender front, fireman's side; handbrake handle and fire-iron tunnel. The paintwork is dotted with chips and scrapes; when you are handling a red-hot 10ft bar the last thing you are worried about is marking the paint! *SHA*

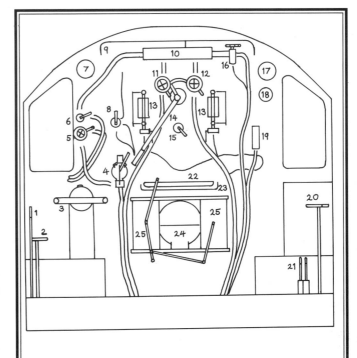

Cab Controls, Class 5X and 5P5F Engines

1	Cylinder cocks	14	Regulator
2	Live injector water regulator	15	Blower
3	Reverser	16	Train heat valve
4	Brake application valve	17	Boiler pressure gauge
5	Large ejector steam	18	Train heat gauge
6	Small ejector steam	19	Continuous blowdown valve
7	Vacuum gauge	20	Exhaust injector water regulator
8	Sander steam valve	21	Dampers
9	Whistle	22	Tray
10	Auxiliary supply turret	23	Glare shield
11	Live injector steam	24	Firedoor flap
12	Exhaust injector steam	25	Firedoors
13	Boiler water gauges		

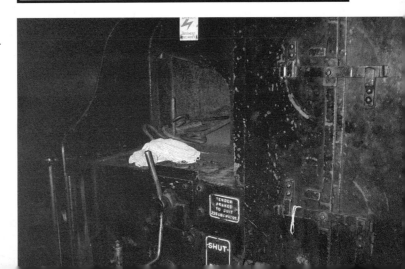

Above:
**Another of Bristol's '5Xs',
No 45660 *Rooke* is seen
under the coal tower at
Holbeck. The external state
of the engine gives away the
truth that this was taken on
29 March 1965, after she had
been moved to Leeds. 'Grade
1' refers to the better class
of coal delivered on that side
for passenger engines.**
G. W. Morrison

Left:
**On the turntable and ready to
leave the shed.**
Ian Allan Library

about 20min, which are as follows: an engine and brake van en route from Carlton to the Calder Valley; 10.48am Ardsley-Stourton; 6.45am Chaddesden (Derby)-Hunslet; 10.50am Wath-Carlton; 11am Manvers Main Colliery-Carlton North Sidings; 9.54am pick-up from Rotherham, shunting at Kilnhurst West; 10.50am Rotherham Masborough Sidings-Mexborough No 1, waiting for the road at Roundwood; 10.30am Masborough Sidings-Carlton North Sidings, pulling away from Masborough passenger station as we pass. This complex tangle of tracks is probably the most intensively used in the country, and we can see why the Midland was a pioneer in central traffic control. From the planners' point of view, the ideal approach to passing the greatest number of trains along a line is to have them all moving at the same speed; with such a variety of traffic this is impossible, but they can compromise by running trains of the same class in bunches. We will be following the 8.15am Newcastle-Cardiff express all the way from Wath Road Junction to Gloucester with a headway of around eight minutes, so our timekeeping is largely dependent on that — except that in the later stages we overhaul the 7.30am Newcastle-Bristol.

Through Kilnhurst the Midland main line is shadowed by the Great Central, sometimes only a few hundred yards to the east. This is sometimes derided as a duplication left over from the days of competition, but in reality it is a valuable asset. The existence of alternatives to nearly every route is the key to the virtue that nothing, not even wartime bombing, has ever stopped our railways. After all, motorists in the vital industrial corridor of the Don valley would not tolerate having only one way through and movement ceasing if that was blocked, so why should railway users be put in such a situation?

Our fireman has not put any coal on since Royston, in anticipation of a temporary permanent way slack near Darfield. We racket over Storrs Mill Junction; southerners may not know the place, but you might have heard of the colliery at the end of the branch: Grimethorpe, of brass band fame. Then comes Houghton Colliery, where we shut off, and the steam from No 45407 ceases at once, showing that our mate is alert, and we coast at 30mph past Dearne Valley Colliery and through the 140yd Cat Hill Tunnel. Checking the

time at Wath Road box we find it is 11.7am, so we are doing well so far. However, the schedule is tighter from here on and we will be lucky to meet the allowance of 15min for the 11 miles into Sheffield. The fireman looks at his fire and is satisfied, so he turns off the injector and sits for a minute while the locomotive is whipped up to speed again. He soon resumes shovelling; reference to the gradient profile will show why.

Past the faded elegance of Rotherham Masborough station, at 15mph we take the bend to Holmes, the long train coming into sight astern. On full regulator she blazes away again, accelerating past Harrison & Camms signalbox. Above the blast is now heard a thumping from the tender, and on looking round we see that a big lump of coal has jammed in the shovelling plate and because it is not yet possible to open the doors the fireman is swinging the coalpick sideways like an old-fashioned miner. He is a big lad and soon knocks it to splinters. He finishes and shuts the fire doors in time to catch the signals at Wincobank, and comes over to the left side to start the live steam injector.

The scenery hereabouts is unrelieved industry: ancient quarries and tips overlaid with solid Victorian mills, ugly modern metal barns, clusters of back-to-backs, corner chippies, filthy streams, pipes, laid out to view as we run along the west side of the Don valley. Dominating all are the steelworks, Oxley's Parkgate works, the Park Gate Iron & Steel Co, the South Yorkshire Chemical works, Stubs' Holmes steelworks, Baker & Bessemer's Brinsworth works, Templeborough Steel Works over by the GC line, and many other heavy metal factories. Most dramatic of all, as we run past Grimesthorpe Junction, on our right is the plant of Thomas Firth & John Brown; a vast cliff with flames licking out of chinks everywhere and at ground level glimpses through doorways of a terrifying inferno within. The more aesthetic among our passengers may be horrified by this land of iron, but think on — you all want your cars and washing machines, your smartly furnished, brightly lit homes. Well, the good things in life have to be made, and this is where they come from. This is where their true cost is undisguised.

A standard Midland/LMS 0-6-0T with a brake van clanks past, on its way from shunting at Upwell Street to Wincobank.

Left:
A keen crew getting under way with a will, at Huddersfield on 25 February 1967, with the sanders on. The vacuum ejector is mounted on the side of the firebox, and a long pipe carries ejected air and steam forward to the smokebox, where they are discharged up the chimney. *K. Hale*

Left:
The Middleton Railway line down to the River Aire passed over this bridge, just north of Hunslet Goods Junction where the North Midland went straight on to its Hunslet Lane terminus. The down 'Thames-Clyde', hauled by No 45615 *Malay States*, is heading for Leeds. *K. Field*

Left:
The site of the Middleton Railway bridge on 8 October 1993. In the background are new coaches parked in the private siding of Hunslet, the last of the great Leeds engine builders. *SHA*

On our left a train of steel plate wagons, the 11.8am from Woodhouse Mill to Firth Brown's sidings, is waiting at Brightside Junction, in Grimesthorpe sidings another goods, 9.5am from Shirebrook, is drawing to a stand, and an '8F' is sending up a volcanic column of smoke as she gets under way with the 11.18am to Gowhole. The original branch line runs through the steelworks to a terminus at Wicker and the present main line diverges right. Here the ground rises and we plunge into a world of blackened stone caves and canyons, with the brake on to bring us down to 10mph before emerging from the Duke of Norfolk's Park Tunnel which brings us out into Sheffield Midland station. This is the largest station on the former Midland Railway, and is a mixture of styles and periods, although the original buildings of 1870 and canopies on the west side are very fine. The canopies on the up side are new, replacing an overall roof recently removed. The problem with this station, as with so many in cities, was finding a site for it, and it is built over what was the confluence of the rivers Sheaf and Porter, which are now piped underneath it. Drivers entering the station are instructed to treat all signals as Block Regulation 5 Warnings, viz they must be ready to stop short of any obstruction, and in fact we are signalled in to Platform 5 by a calling-on arm, without stopping as it is exempt from Rule 44(a). We are well on time and should sight the Newcastle-Cardiff train, due out at the time we are due in; it will be the train over on the right, which moves off just after we stop. All we have to do now is bring these 17 vehicles, all with differing braking performances, to a halt within a foot or so of the right spot, by admitting air to a pipe at this end and judging its effect, allowing for a time lag, as it percolates to the back end 300yd away. Doing it right draws the engine up by a water column. The fireman climbs on to the back of the tender to put the hose in while the driver turns the water on. No 45407's driver strolls up.

'Will you be all right for water at Derby?'
'Ar.'

Back in the cab to shut the injector off, she now has a full boiler, a big fire and near maximum pressure ready for the big climb to Dronfield. This is where the line passes through the well-heeled residential parts of Sheffield, through the fringe of the limestone hills, but you do not see much of them as it is mostly in cutting. On the

through road alongside comes the characteristic dry cough of the '8F', and we can count the load she is about to lift up that climb: 48 wagons, about 600 tons.

Getting the right-away on time at 11.29am, we take the load away under the long bridge, the fireman looking back to watch the train out of the station. Then open her up to full regulator and 35% cut-off and leave it at that. As speed gradually rises we come up on the goods train again, and can count it in reverse order until we reach the engine, trundling steadily along, driver leaning imperturbably on his window sill, enjoying the spectacle of the two 4-6-0s putting heart and soul into it. Firing becomes a little harder, coal disappearing into the pure white glare, the heat flaying face and hands, the tender snaking from side to side as No 45407 shakes it in her extreme effort. After 10min of this pounding, Dore & Totley is reached and we take the left fork, past the overspill carriage sidings at South Junction, empty at this time of year, and into Bradway Tunnel. The driver reaches up and puts the sand handle over; these tunnels are notoriously wet and provide all the water used for locomotive supplies in Sheffield. With that and the gradient, Bradway and Totley tunnels are considered so hazardous that they have an unusual protection device in the form of a wire strung along each side which, when broken, sounds an alarm bell in the signalbox ahead. Now the engine subjects us to an even worse battering in the form of noise. On top of the hammering of the exhaust, the safety valves lift, in this confined space so loud that the sound breaks up in our heads to a numbing vibration; but the fireman does not fumble in slamming both injectors full on and shutting the firedoors, so that the noise and heat are reduced to a level which the average person would find merely intolerable. As *Alberta* charges headlong into blackness you should now be convinced, if you were not before, that enginemen are very far from being average people.

After a mile and 267yd, at last daylight and the summit, and we can put the blower on and ease the engine, and take stock. We have about half a glass of water and steam is on 200lb, but the fire has gone well down. However, it will do until after Chesterfield, and with the feed shut off she comes round rapidly. It is time for a cup of tea while she coasts down through a deep cutting and out past Dronfield

Colliery. Here a down goods is attaching wagons on its way to Earle's Sidings in the Hope Valley. There are several mines in this valley, served by a loop line that rejoins the main route near Unstone. Further down the view opens out once more, the elevation of Unstone viaduct making a change from long deep cuttings. We seem to be going at an absolutely breakneck speed until the brake has to be put on to steady her. A branch line leading to the great Sheepbridge Iron Works passes beneath, and the original main line appears below to the left; now braking in earnest, we drop into it at Tapton Junction. At this point No 45407 starts blowing off vigorously and gives us a push. Our driver, from his side window, conducts a discourse that conveys by quite unofficial gestures his views on fire-brands who show off and display unnecessary enthusiasm. There is no authorised method of communication between crews when double-heading, apart from the universal one of three short pops on the whistle which means 'Hit the brake'.

On our left, out of sight over the nearby hill, is Tapton House, George Stephenson's final home, where the great man spent his sadly brief retirement enjoying his pets and greenhouses and taking an interest in the trains passing his grounds. He was buried at Holy Trinity Church in north Chesterfield. That is not the one which dominates the view of the town — the Parish Church with the grotesque bent spire. It is 8ft out of true at the tip and is the sole agency giving the place an entry in absolutely every topographical book, doubtless the reason why no one has the temerity to suggest mending it.

A single heavy brake application brings us to an abrupt stop at Chesterfield, and there is comparatively little activity on the platform, so they wave us away in under a minute and actually ahead of time at about 11.52am. The pause is enlivened by the passage at speed of the 7.35am Bristol-Bradford working, hauled by one of the new Standard Class 5s being given a real leathering. Here we finally part company with the rivals, two Great Central lines going over and under at a three-tier intersection. The driver has a spell of firing, just to keep fit, ending up with a black mass up to the ring extending about a third of the way down the box. This looks like a bit of a surfeit for poor *Alberta*, but

she has to be pushed fairly hard up to Clay Cross and steams well on it. As she leans to the fast 60mph curve through Clay Cross he shuts the doors, taps his mate on the shoulder and shouts: 'Right, shut up the shop. Lunch hour'.

Few places less relaxing than the mile of Dantean darkness of Clay Cross Tunnel can be imagined, yet in the firelight the fireman makes a brew of tea, produces some rolls and a paper screw of butter, and as she dashes out into the sunlight both men make a swift meal with every indication of comfort. All the time their attention never strays far from their responsibilities, one watching the road and the other adjusting dampers and injector, flicking a couple of rounds on the fire and periodically blowing down the boiler water gauges. In pleasant countryside the engine gallops happily away over Stretton summit. On the hillside above us is the course of a curiosity, the Ashover Light Railway, opened in 1925 and closed just 25 years later, built to carry ore from Ashover quarries to Clay Cross Iron Works. The latter was founded by George Stephenson; while working on the tunnel in 1837 he noted that both coal and iron lay below ground, and set up in business to exploit them. He also used the coal in kilns at Ambergate, burning lime from quarries at nearby Crich, and the whole enterprise proved a nice little money-spinner. The station at Wingfield, designed by the North Midland's tame architect Francis Thompson, is said to be a fine example. South of Lodge Hill Tunnel (250yd) comes Bull Bridge, another three-level structure where the railway passes over the River Amber and under the Cromford Canal. We do not see the unusual triple station on Ambergate's triangular junction, as it has a bypass taking us through a tunnel. Crossing over the River Derwent immediately afterwards, we race through another tunnel which, owing to the unstable structure of the hill above, is lined with iron rings. This is common modern practice but was very advanced for the 1830s. Shortly after comes a cutting through Belper, named from Beau Repaire, the Earl of Lancaster's hunting-lodge, but an industrial town since Joseph Strutt built his cotton mill in 1776. Then we cross the river again and charge into another long tunnel, Milford at 836yd.

At this time the general racket of the engine is overlaid by the sound of a Somerset burr voicing an impressive range

Above:
Seen from the road bridge at Normanton on 2 July 1966, Class 5P5F No 45080 is pictured on the main line with an up goods, passing the locomotive depot. In front of the shed are LMS concrete coal and ash plants, the original coal stage being down the far end of the yard. By the tail of the train is Normanton North signalbox, and in the distance the buildings and winding gears of West Riding Colliery.
G. W. Morrison

Centre right:
On the same evening as the previous view, Normanton station, and once more we have to ask you to forgive the diesel train. Class 8F No 48202 clanks past with an up goods. The second wagon is a 'hood' with a central bar over which a tarpaulin may be fixed. *G. W. Morrison*

Right:
In Sheffield's back yard; view from a train passing the Templeborough Steel Works on the Great Central line, on 15 September 1979. *SHA*

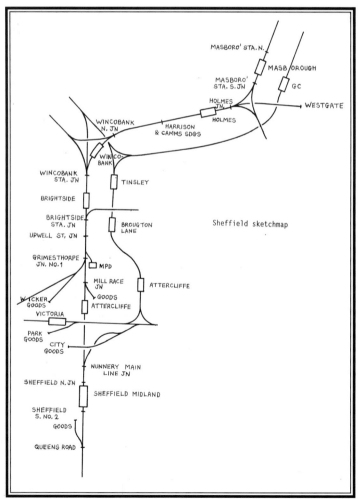

Sheffield sketchmap

MASBORO' STA. N.

MASBOROUGH

MASBORO' STA. S. JN

GC

HOLMES JN.

HOLMES

WESTGATE

WINCOBANK N. JN

HARRISON & CAMMS SDGS

WINCOBANK

WINCOBANK STA. JN

TINSLEY

BRIGHTSIDE

BRIGHTSIDE STA. JN

BROUGTON LANE

UPWELL ST, JN

GRIMESTHORPE JN. NO.1

MPD

MILL RACE JN

ATTERCLIFFE

WICKER GOODS

GOODS ATTERCLIFFE

VICTORIA

PARK GOODS

CITY GOODS

NUNNERY MAIN LINE JN

SHEFFIELD N. JN

SHEFFIELD MIDLAND

SHEFFIELD S. NO. 2

GOODS

QUEENS ROAD

of basic epithets. The fireman has been hosing down the coal and the floor, and a lurch of the engine has made him spray his legs and feet with boiling water. Fortunately it did not hit any exposed skin as he has his dungarees tied round his ankles. Even on a hot day it is advisable to be well covered against such an encounter. A steam engine is a bit like a sailing ship: while not overtly hostile, she makes no allowances and given a moment's inattention she is likely to bite.

The lurch was only natural, as we are doing a good 70mph, up to the limit over Duffield Junction. With the footplate cleaned, a fire blacked out at the back and sloping away to the front, 210lb on the clock and half a glass of water we are all shipshape to present ourselves in Derby.

Derby is not a railway-created town, although the Midland works, dating from 1840 and now covering 210 acres, form the oldest and biggest railway establishment. Because of its position it has been a key point in communication and military strategy since Roman times. Here Prince Charles Edward Stuart arrived from the north on 4 December 1745 and held a council which made the fateful decision to turn back. In industry it has a reputation for quality manufacture, such as the Lombe silk mill of 1717, Crown Derby China of 1750 and the Rolls-Royce car factory set up in 1907. The railway works occupy the area that nobody else wanted between the town and the river. Their products can be seen hauling trains anywhere from Bournemouth to Wick, but their wide application does not negate the gross inadequacies in their design, and the fact remains that as the technical centre of the one-time biggest company in the world,

the London Midland & Scottish Railway, Derby failed to provide it with motive power fit for the 20th century. The works has just completed what may be their last steam locomotive, a Standard Class 5 No 73154.

On our approach we find all signals on at St Mary's and finally come to a stand at the North Junction, where a branch goes left to the main freight marshalling yard at Chaddesden. A hold-up at this busy spot is not surprising, with the traffic in and out of the yard; probably a trip movement or the 12 noon empties to Dovefields has blocked us. Fortunately it is only a brief stop, as No 45407's crew are getting a bit anxious about water. On being cleared we run through the station, brake almost to a stop and, putting on the large ejector for a quick release, roll on a few feet before snapping the brake on to spot the hinder engine right for the column. For the moment we have nothing to do and can watch some other engines; a 'Doodlebug' (Ivatt 2-6-0) arriving with the 9.37am empty stock train from Crewe, a 'Baby Austin' (Derby 0-8-0) with the 12.10pm Chaddesden-New Lount coal empties rumbling along the goods line and a parallel-boiler 2-6-4T preparing to take the 12.45pm passenger train to Walsall. While this goes on the 'Devonian' undergoes a change — from an up train to a down train. The convention is that the Down direction is always away from London, so in travelling past the capital we are bound to change somewhere. This usage is unfamiliar to non-railway folk who are used to seeing north at the top of the map, but it is of course vital to have a clear definition of

Below left:
Alberta **on the climb south-wards from Sheffield with the Saturday Bradford-Poole through train on 9 July 1966. This was in the period when some of Holbeck's engines were officially allocated to nearby Farnley Junction depot.** *L. A. Nixon*

Right:
On 4 July 1961 the Newcastle-Bristol through train has 'Royal Scot' No 46157 **The Royal Artilleryman** **making a good start on the climb from Sheffield past Millhouses signalbox.** *J. M. Smith*

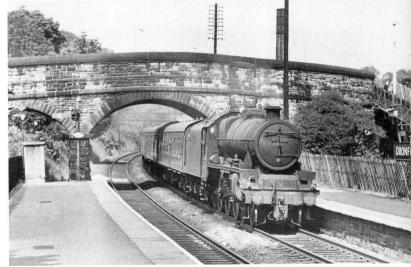

Right:
Over the top and steam is shut off, and **Alberta** **gathers speed through Dronfield.** *L. A. Nixon*

Right:
A typical coal train, at least 40 wagons hauled by '8F' No 48150, at Tapton Junction, coming off the old main line, on 29 April 1963. *D. Booth*

direction on any route, and all that matters is that everyone knows what it is. *Alberta* draws our attention to herself by blowing-off suddenly, which we silence with the injector. It is 12.34pm by the time the guard gives us the office, and we start briskly away, but almost at once there is another check. The fireman has started to shovel, but he leaves off, opens the doors and turns the blower on to reduce the smoke with which we smother the laundry at Melbourne Junction (Melbourne is famous as the birthplace of Thomas Cook, inventor of the excursion train). Ahead at Stenson things have got clogged. Two freights, the 9.45am Washwood Heath-Toton and the 11.55am Burton Wetmore-Toton, have to cross our line, an empty from Willington power station has to get across to the upside, the 11.25am Toton-Leamington Spa service is due to shunt clear at 12.28pm, and then the Cardiff train and ours have to be passed while the 8.30am Cardiff-Newcastle working is due through the other way. It does not take much to put everybody behind time in these circumstances. Once more we stop, and get away some seven minutes behind time. But now we are right away to Birmingham, and make full use of the ample power at our disposal in a sustained surge of acceleration up to 70mph on a level road.

The power station dominates the modern view here, but the village of Repton beyond it was once a very important place, no less than the capital of the kingdom of Mercia. Its school, founded in 1854, has a Southern Railway engine named after it, and nearby Foremarke Hall, also part of the school, has a Great Western engine named after it! However, a couple more miles take us to a place more important and interesting from our point of view: Burton upon Trent.

Even if you never touch beer, do not dismiss its contribution to the nation. Two hundred years ago clean water was not on tap; if life was to be made longer and more productive something disease-free to drink had to be provided on a large scale, and brewing was the answer. It was a carrier, William Bass, who recognised that transport was the key to development, and when the Trent & Mersey Canal opened in 1777 he began brewing here. In 1862 the Guild Street branch was built, the first of a network of railway lines that took material in and out of the breweries and other industries without transhipment to road wagons. Eventually Bass, Worthington, Ind Coope & Allsopp, Branston Artificial Silk, Lloyds Foundry, Marston Thompson Evershed, Thomas Salt, Charringtons, Trumans and the Burton Brewery all had their own sidings worked by their own engines. Local firm Thornewill & Warham built 66 engines for local use, and Baguley Cars Ltd built diesel shunters and railcars. By far the largest user was Bass Ratcliffe & Gretton, who designed their own engines and ran their system to a timetable with a central control. Controlling the country-wide movement of ale casks alone employed an office of 35 men. Today the Bass-Worthington system has 21 engines working on 22 miles of track and also running on the main line through Burton station. The attraction to railway enthusiasts of this town with its 32 level crossings is obvious, but its wider importance is that it explodes the fallacy that commerce needs for its prosecution the unfettered use of road transport. There is no case for massive road widening and lorries passing everyone's front door; railway tracks can link every part of our industry, and Burton is the proof of it.

Burton station is an island platform round which the main lines snake with a 30mph limit, so the brake is hard on as we pass Wetmore ale bank. Here the 9.55am Tibshelf-Aston service is 'lifting and leaving' and one of the little Midland four-wheeled tank engines is doing a shunt into Old Dixie Sidings under the eye of that stern official the Old Dixie Inspector. Under Horninglow bridge we overtake an 0-6-0 on a coal train, the 10.55am from Chaddesden Yard to Branston sidings for Drakelow power station — a new installation that came on line in 1955. Then both our engines erupt into full power again to get up speed as quickly as possible. Every minute or so the fireman flashes eight shovels of coal into the box. There is plenty of steam. The regulator is wide open and the reverser on 30%. Over the great River Trent on Wichnor viaduct the gradient becomes slightly up and we give her another notch. On No 45407 the driver checks the second intermediate block signal after Elford and shouts across:

'Shut the dampers and doors and put the blower on. He'll have his scoop in.'

Seconds later a cloud of spray souses the engine as *Alberta* picks up water from Tamworth trough, and as it clears we are

One of the wartime versions of the '8F', sometimes called 'WD', No 90706 hauls coal empties north from Chesterfield on 24 July 1967. The notorious crooked spire of the town's parish church is at top right. *J. S. Hancock*

Not all summer days are cheerful. At the south end of Chesterfield Midland on a June day in 1965, the road is clear on the up main, while on the goods lines a Ministry of Supply 2-8-0 makes laboured progress towards Hollis Lane, just visible in the murk. *S. Tallis*

Above:
Although it is not on the
direct 'Devonian' route, here
is part of the triple station at
Ambergate. This is the north-
south side, with '5P5F'
No 45006, still with a dome
less boiler, working the
5.26pm Sheffield-Derby stopping train on 27 April 1963.
Behind the tail of the train is
the end of the west-north
side. Motorists may also wax
nostalgic over the Hillman
Minx in the forecourt.
A. W. Smith

Left:
Another engine type seen on
the 'Devonian' was the BR
Standard Class 5. No 73068
leaves Derby with the down
train (which has just been
up) on 21 April 1955. The
state of this three-year old
engine, filthy and with a
blowing gland, typifies the
squalid, run-down image of
British Railways at this time.
Some money spent on cleaning up their act would have
been a good investment.
A. N. Yeates

screaming through the high level station and along the Anker viaduct. Five minutes later both firemen put down their shovels and straighten their backs, thinking that if these engines are to come off at Birmingham it is time to think about working the fire down.

We are entering another region of mines, quarries and brickworks and at Kingsbury is a yard where two goods trains are making ready to leave: the 1.13pm to Whitacre and 1.20pm to Coleshill. Here the fast lines bear to the right on a cut-off which leaves the original route and rejoins it at Water Orton. The curves are taken at speed. For several miles have been in sight ahead the towers of another power station complex, Hams Hall. For the travel-book writers who dismiss them as eye-sores, the same goes as for other industrial plant — if you like having the electricity, you should appreciate the source of it.

Whistle sounding, we shoot under the bridge at Water Orton and past a yard used as a concentration point for freight traffic clear of the congested and over-worked depots of Birmingham. To our right is the famous Castle Bromwich aircraft factory where Spitfires were built, now

occupied by Morris Motors. It is followed by the vast railway sidings of Washwood Heath, with on the other side the works of the biggest firm hereabouts, Metropolitan Cammell Carriage & Wagon Co.

Our route through Birmingham is, as elsewhere, a conglomeration of lines built quite separately: the Birmingham & Derby terminating at Lawley Street; the Birmingham & Gloucester at Camp Hill; the Birmingham West Suburban from Lifford to Granville Street; and, finally, links put in when the Midland was invited to join the London & North Western's new station site at New Street. Through running via New Street only became possible in 1885 when a link was built to the BWSR at Church Road Junction. The route to Lawley Street branches off opposite Saltley locomotive depot, the principal Midland shed. Here the Camp Hill line enters on an abrupt climb, but it merely serves to slow down the train without braking. The tracks split again, then we turn right under the LNWR and up a steep ramp, 1 in 58, to join it. Climbing continues under a bridge carrying the Great Western line on its way into Snow Hill Tunnel, and into a tunnel of our own, 238yd long.

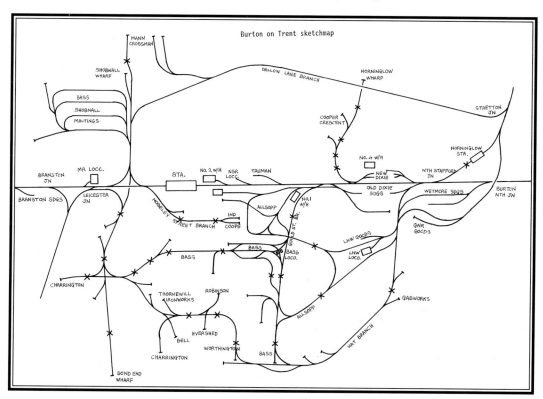

Burton on Trent sketchmap

Top:
From the Old Dixie Sidings, one of the 2-6-0s designed at Horwich for the LMS, No 42763, starts away with the 6.50pm freight to London. *R. C. Riley*

Above
No 45636 *Uganda* **picking up water at speed.** *P. H. Groom*

Below left:
BR Class 9 2-10-0 No 92051 from Saltley passing Water Orton station just after starting from Water Orton marshalling yard on the long haul to Carlisle with the 4.55pm service. This was one of the most demanding locomotive jobs in the country.
P. Ransome-Wallis

Above:
On the run into Birmingham we pass another haul of coal empties back to the mines. The wagons are behind Midland 0-6-0 No 44562, rumbling through Castle Bromwich on 4 May 1963.
G. T. Robinson

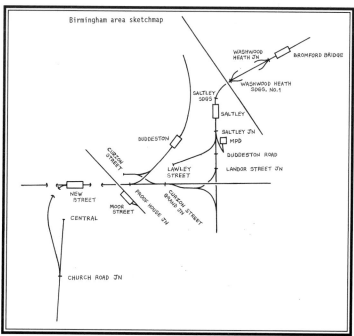

Birmingham area sketchmap

WASHWOOD HEATH JN — BROMFORD BRIDGE
WASHWOOD HEATH SDGS. NO.1
SALTLEY SDGS
SALTLEY
SALTLEY JN
MPD
DUDDESTON
DUDDESTON ROAD
LANDOR STREET JN
CURZON STREET
LAWLEY STREET
NEW STREET
MOOR STREET
PROOF HOUSE JN
CURZON STREET GRAND JN
CENTRAL
CHURCH ROAD JN

This route takes us round to the south side of the acropolis that is Birmingham city centre, where the station is set in as close as possible, in an excavation, made dark by the walls hemming it in, which manages to be pretty gloomy on even the brightest day. As in many places, there are actually two stations, separated by Queen's Drive. The LNW station, the northern part, opened in 1854, and the Midland station in 1885; the eastern approach remained a two-track bottleneck until 1893. Years of intensive use, ugly surrounding buildings and war damage have since taken their toll of this gateway to England's second city.

An army of signals demands our attention here, for in the space of 2½ miles are seven signalboxes: Washwood Heath Sidings No 1, Saltley Sidings, Saltley Junction, Duddeston Road, Landor Street Junction, Curzon Street Grand Junction and Proof House Junction. Since a train takes only about five minutes to run past them, it has to be belled through in advance on the block instruments, and further bell signals passed along the line to track its approach, so as we cruise along at about 30mph the signalmen will be talking volubly to each other on their telegraphs in their language of bell strokes. In front of us, signal arms rise to beckon us through, and all four men watch to see that all is right and safe. The hard steaming needed to lift the train up the climb keeps the fire hot, and from habit the fireman starts the live steam injector in the tunnel. Shutting off steam, we roll into the left-hand platform, No 10. The Cardiff train is here on No 9, a lighter 10-coach load headed by a single '5X', although it is timed to leave at the moment we arrive and does not make a connection. However, our eyes are on the sidings at the far end where we hope to see our own engines from Bristol, and there they are, in the dock just beside where we pull up.

Below:
Down in New Street station, you felt you were in a man-made canyon. Class 5P5F No 45020 was photographed running into the Midland side on 25 October 1952. *Ian Allan Library*

Right:
An aerial view of Birmingham New Street shows the contrast between the LNW station, which lost its roof in 1940, and the Midland station. New Street is the roadway down the left of the picture. *BICC Ltd*

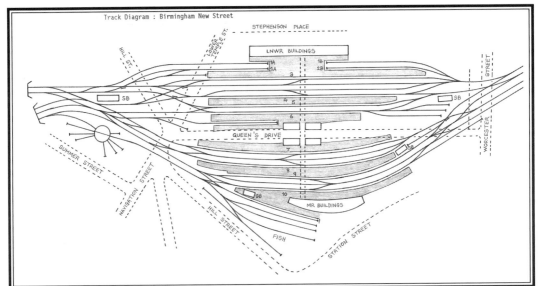

Track Diagram : Birmingham New Street

Devonian

Birmingham to Bristol

On the platform end four enginemen and a shunter are standing, and one — a man in his sixties who has become unfit for main line work, the others being youngsters just passed out — swings on to our footplate.

'Hey up lads, there's your machines. Gather your traps and we'll take these off for you.'

We pick up our bags, jackets and tea can, not forgetting the shovel, and walk across to the leading engine. She is No 45690 *Leander*. She is largely similar to *Alberta*, built at Crewe in March 1936 as one of the final batch. As a popular and well-used engine on the long-distance turns, she is racking up the miles pretty steadily and is already roughening up a little. Her last spell in works was in November-December 1956 for an Intermediate repair, following a General in September 1955. (Works overhauls are graded as General, Intermediate or Casual with further division into Heavy or Light.) The companion engine, No 45662 *Kempenfelt*, completes a trio by being built at Derby, whence she was released on 28 December 1934. (Kempenfelt was an 18th century admiral responsible for home defence during the War of American Independence.) She also has been through a General in 1955, an Intermediate in May 1956 and a Casual in October 1956, and like *Leander* is due for consideration for 'Shopping' when this summer is over. It is a fact of railway life that the best engines get the most use, and a shedmaster who has a duff one on his hands has a running battle to get enough miles on it to ratify its acceptance to Works.

Leander and *Kempenfelt* have been at Bristol since allocation on 19 October 1947; they and *Rooke*, *Galatea*, *Jervis*, *Barfleur* and *Trafalgar* are the pride and joy

Above left:
Our train engine from Birmingham, No 45662 *Kempenfelt*. This portrait was taken in a remote outpost of the Midland empire; backing on to a train at York, under Holgate Bridge. The cattle wagons are standing at Holgate cattle dock. *E. Treacy*

of the top link at the Barrow Road depot.

On boarding *Leander* we see the glass is full, the pressure near the red line and a big sloping fire. She has been cleaned, the boiler backhead wiped down and the coal damped — every appearance of a good preparation. The other engines have already disappeared and without ado we spin the handbrake off, our driver creates the brake, blows the whistle, is answered from behind, and moves off on to the turntable road. The shunting disc flicks over and we are backing on to the train, checking the antics of the vacuum gauge as we go. All this is done without any hesitation, for the driver knows the track layout and signalling here as well as all the others on the route. Braking almost to a stop six feet off, the shunter beckons us back and we ease up just hard enough to compress the buffers slightly. Test the brake after he has coupled up and we are ready to go at 1.33pm.

Because of the curvature the platform side of the train is out of our sight, so an illuminated sign is provided, showing an 'R' when activated by the guard. Pulling out of New Street we pass close by *Alberta* and No 45407 standing on the engine spur, and enter Suffolk Street tunnel. This is on a 1 in 80 gradient and a sharp curve and at full first valve and 60% our progress is noisy and slow, working in an opaque smoky fog while passengers grumble and pull shut their windows. According to normal routine we wait until the end of the steep pitch before opening the doors and firing a round, then getting the exhaust injector going, then another round, and so on, and soon she is getting into her stride and the driver is pulling her up. There are speed limits: 20mph in the first tunnel, 40mph at Church Road Junction, 50mph through Selly Oak and 35mph round the curve to Kings Norton, so we have time to study the uninviting water of the Worcester & Birmingham Canal close alongside. Here is Bournville, perhaps the most famous company town in the country; it was open country until 1879 when Cadbury built its

Above left:
The last '5P5F' built, No 44687, had a double chimney, roller-bearing axleboxes and British-Caprotti poppet valves. She is seen after arriving at New Street with an extra from Manchester on 15 June 1957.
Ian Allan Library

Below left:
No 45690 *Leander*: this view was taken on 20 October 1979, after the engine had been preserved and rebuilt, hence the LMS livery and exhibition finish. Contrast the new wheel tyres on this engine with the worn-out tyres in the views of *Alberta* in her last days. *R. Payne*

Above right:
The first Great Western engine met with is as likely as not to be a pannier tank. This is '94xx' class No 8480 of Worcester shed.
Ian Allan Library

Centre right:
At Bromsgrove on a bright winter day, 6 January 1957. The bankers on duty, Nos 92079 and 8402, have a siding on the up side with a coaling stage. Across the main lines and goods loops is South signalbox, with a mess hut for engine crews changing trains here. Note the clinker shovel and dart hanging on the bunker of the pannier tank. Both engines are carrying red tail lights. *H. C. Casserley*

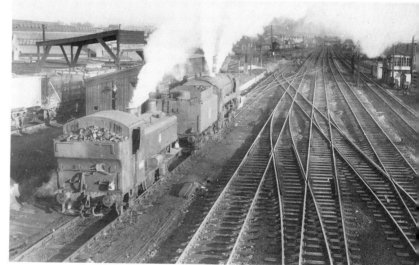

Right:
Pannier tank No 8403 departs from Bromsgrove banking a train formed of five LMSR coaches and an LNER van. A down goods approaches, signalled through the station platform and into the goods loop, where it will stop at South signalbox and take water while the brakes are released. *H. C. Casserley*

factory on the up side by Stirchley Street station. Its railway system has six miles of track, crossing over the main line to a wharf, sends out three trains a day and its engines are, of course, chocolate-coloured. Further on at Halesowen Junction is another factory with a familiar name, the Austin Motor Co.

Something is wrong. *Leander* was almost blowing-off at the start, but now steam is down to 190lb and is not recovering as it should after the initial effort. The fireman checks that the damper is full open and puts his shovel, inverted, into the firehole so that it deflects the flames and gives him a sight of the fire itself. He also peers in to see if the brick arch is intact. He shuts off the injector and gives it another couple of minutes. Finally he crosses to the driver.

'I think we've got a cold one, mate.'

He means that the engine is not steaming. This confronts the driver with a dilemma. It could be argued that his use of the engine controls is solely directed to timing the train, producing steam as he requires it being the other man's job, and there are drivers around who work on that basis, but the driving can influence the steaming and the true engineman recognises this. When steam is short the natural reaction would be to ease the engine and reduce consumption, but doing so will reduce the blast on the fire and might make it worse. The remedy is more likely to be to open up in order to make the fire burn more freely. It depends partly on the nature of the fault; somewhere in the leaping flames, violently boiling water and hundredweights of dancing rods is the problem, and he thinks it over without relaxing his attention to the road. It is probably not mechanical, as she has an even beat, the big-end impacts are normal and the ride is to '5X' standard, harsh but steady. He does not criticise the firing — you do not get on these jobs unless you are a top-class professional. However, the fire could have been badly prepared, in which case it should improve, and we do have the luxury of another engine to help out. 'We'll be all right with them behind. See how it goes till we're down Lickey.'

The Lickey Incline is perhaps chiefly famous for being famous, as it is not an especially severe piece of railway. It is, however, exceptional in being accessible to the public, located in pleasant pastoral surroundings and on a main line on which all classes of trains are regularly worked,

and is made more spectacular by being dead straight. It extends for 2 miles 7 chains, on an average gradient of 1 in 37.7, attaining in one bound 292ft of the rise between the River Severn flood plain and the central watershed of the Midlands; this is the rise that the Worcester & Birmingham Canal surmounts by the Tardebigge flight of 42 locks.

It was designed in this form by William Moorsom in 1835, and was originally projected for self-acting rope haulage. Within a couple of years, though, Moorsom decided it should be worked by locomotives, a revolutionary idea then notwithstanding the pace of locomotive development in those days. Indeed, no British manufacturer would quote for the job and it was an American firm, Norris of Philadelphia, which promised a suitable machine. (This early example of the Americans re-exporting back to Britain something the British had lately invented and given to them was an unpleasant pointer to things to come.) The Norris design did not meet the specification and they had to build a 'special' for use on the incline, thus inaugurating a family of dedicated Lickey Bankers. *Great Britain*, designed and built in the B & G works at Bromsgrove in 1845, was then the biggest locomotive in the country; then until last year they had the lovely 'Big Bertha'. Although she was only 36 years old and had two boilers, they were both worn out and with the decision to discard steam power already taken, there was no point in building another. Her place was taken by a BR Standard 2-10-0, No 92079. The change also drew attention to the age of the Midland standard tanks which worked the bank, as a result of which Bromsgrove took on loan from the Western Region six fairly new pannier tanks.

Since the 9.45am Bournemouth-Manchester 'Pines Express' is due to ascend the Lickey while the 'Devonian' is descending, we thought we might join one of the engines pushing it up. No 92079 is in works at present, so what we find standing in the bankers' siding by Bromsgrove South signalbox is pannier tank No 8404. She was delivered in September 1949 by the Yorkshire Engine Co, and after her second overhaul in June 1956 was based at Newton Abbot until loaned to Bromsgrove on 8 November. The allocation was made permanent on 27 January 1957.

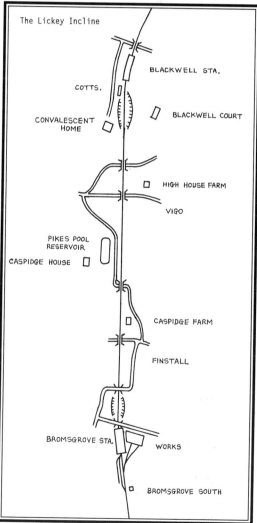

The Lickey Incline

BLACKWELL STA.

COTTS.

CONVALESCENT HOME

BLACKWELL COURT

HIGH HOUSE FARM

VIGO

PIKES POOL RESERVOIR

CASPIDGE HOUSE

CASPIDGE FARM

FINSTALL

BROMSGROVE STA.

WORKS

BROMSGROVE SOUTH

Above:
Freight trains are given assisting engines according to their weight, and this oil train from Fawley refinery to Bromford Bridge, Birmingham, has four: Nos 8402, 8409, 9493 and 8480. They are not coupled together.
A. McBlain

Below:
We have travelled all this way without picturing one of the legendary Midland Compounds, so here is No 1058 starting away from Bromsgrove with a stopping train to Worcester on 26 June 1948. To the right is the engine shed, part of the works complex.
P. F. Twine

Left:
On the up line at Abbots Wood we see one of the oil trains from Fawley refinery to Bromford Bridge. The date is 3 May 1964. The grimy state of the 2-10-0 gives no hint that just over three years previously she was presented to the public as something special: No 92220 *Evening Star* — the last steam locomotive built for British Railways. *C. Roberts*

Left:
A Cardiff-Birmingham Snow Hill train passes Lansdown Junction, Cheltenham in April 1956. The engine, ex-GWR 'Hall' class No 6918 *Sandon Hall*, is in BR black livery. Behind her are the tracks to Lansdown station. The tracks diverging to the left go to the MSWJ.
P. Ransome-Wallis

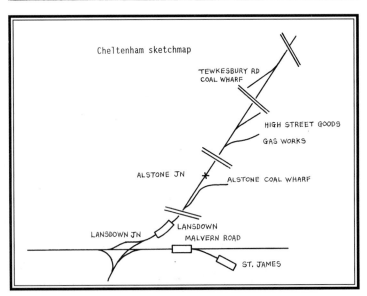

Right:
Between Cheltenham and Gloucester there are many instances of trains timed very close together, and here are two at Elm Bridge box. Class 5P5F No 44966 is on a Midland Bradford-Bristol express and 'Hall' No 4991 *Cobham Hall* is on a Wolverhampton-Ilfracombe service. It is a pity that both engines are so filthy as to inculcate distaste, but that was normal in the early 1960s. *G. England*

The maximum unassisted load allowed up is four coaches or eight wagons. The load of each passenger train is wired to Bromsgrove and bankers are provided accordingly. A driver who wants more assistance than the formula lays down, and all freight trains, must whistle up at Stoke Works Junction, one short followed by the number of bankers wanted. The train stops at an indicator in rear of Bromsgrove station up home, or wherever is needed to clear the crossovers at the back, unless it is calling at the station, when the bankers are brought on in the platform. The bankers are not coupled to the train.

The 'Pines' with a tare load below 370 tons rates two bankers and they make up their fires about 10min before it arrives. Within seconds of the back end coming to a stop on the main line the shunting disc moves and No 8404 chuffs briskly over and the driver buffers her up very gently against the coach. Moments later there is a slight jar as a second engine comes on behind us. Each driver then gives two 'crow' whistles — peeep-pip-peeep-pip-peeep — which the distant train engine repeats. A pause, then another 'crow' from the front end, at which full forward gear is selected, and a short whistle, whereupon both banker drivers open their regulators, for the train driver is starting. It is not unknown for the bankers to be left behind on starting, which can be awkward since if they do not go with the train the latter is, technically, divided, and if they chase after it there is a risk of colliding with it. Acceleration is very quick through the station until the whole train is on the bank and the speed settles to about 22mph. The roar of the blast through our firehole contrasts with a sharp bark from the chimney just behind, the two not keeping in phase because although both engines have the same wheel size in theory, in practice they can be up to an inch different, according to the state of wear of the tyres. For the first few yards there is a terrific eruption of smoke as the blast pulls the coal tar out of the fresh fire, but this quickly diminishes as the fire is whipped into white heat. Pressure falls at first, then comes up to the 200lb red line, demanding use of the injector to avoid wasting steam. Halfway up the incline, the engine is getting so hot and the exhaust steam is coming out at such a lick, that it never condenses in the dry summer air and nothing at all is visible above the chimney. What matters now is

not efficiency but force, so she is kept in full gear, with regulator about half open and the driver repeatedly pulling it up a little more until, nearing the top, the sound beating back from the cutting sides is glorious. Speed increases and Blackwell station appears, but No 8404 is kept hard at it until the barking behind ceases and the other engine drops back; only then does our driver shut off and brake gently to a halt. He then sets back slowly and propels the other over a crossover and up to the down advance starter at the top of the bank. A call-on arm is provided here for the bankers, and when it comes off, with an indicator showing a 'W' to warn that shunting is blocking Bromsgrove station, both engines, still not coupled together, move gently away down the hill.

Back on the 'Devonian', *Leander's* fireman allows his fire to burn down. The pick is brought into play to break all large coal to four-inch size, he fires half-shovelfuls alternately to left and right, front and back, shutting the doors between each one, and the injector is cut back. This means he is working continuously, but he manages to keep her on 180lb until the driver shuts off for Blackwell. He promptly puts the blower

Below:
The view from the east end of Gloucester Eastgate station. No 45056 arrives with the 12.15pm train from Birmingham on 16 October 1957. The rear of the train has just cleared Tramway Junction. To the right are three sidings, the goods loops and Gloucester Goods Junction signalbox. *P. J. Sharpe*

on full and opens up the injector. All trains have to observe a 10mph limit at Blackwell and Bromsgrove and take not less than five minutes to descend the incline, while unfitted goods trains stop to put down the wagon brakes and must take not less than 12min to descend. On the way down the driver, who has informed *Kempenfelt's* crew by sign language that they will have to do most of the work, looks over. 'How're you doing?'

'Well, so-so. Could be blocked tubes or ashpan, but it was all right yesterday. Might do better if you work her a bit heavy.'

'All right. If necessary we'll stop and change the engines round.'

He does not elaborate, but he has in mind that even though *Leander* can get through if she can make enough steam to move herself she may not be able to work the brakes, in which case the solution will be to place *Kempenfelt* in front so that she takes on the task. He opens up again and with his mate's ultra-careful firing and the blower on all the time, pressure slowly goes back while the water gradually drops, but with the road tending downhill it is tolerable. The train is flying along at 75mph and by Ashchurch we are on time.

Stoke Works Junction is where a connection branches off to join the Oxford, Worcester & Wolverhampton line, and a link where the latter crosses over the B & G at Abbots Wood enables trains on our route to call at Worcester. The 'Works' is a salt extraction plant, founded in 1830 by

Above:
**At Tramway Junction on
3 October 1964 is the 1.25am
Tees Yard-Cardiff service. It
is pictured running from
Barnwood Curve to Central
station. The tracks in front of
it are the South Junction-
Eastgate connection and the
wagon works headshunt. The
white patches on engine
No 92070 are the result of
water hardness, which has
oozed from the safety valves,
regulator gland and snifting
valve. Behind her is the ex-
GWR engine shed.**
G. T. Robinson

Right:
**The famous *Evening Star*
again, this time on the
7.30am Gloucester-Bristol
all-stations local on 1 August
1964. The locomotive is seen
pulling out of Wickwar station towards the tunnel. At
least one passenger appears
to be aware of the incon-
gruity of the motive power.**
W. L. Underhay

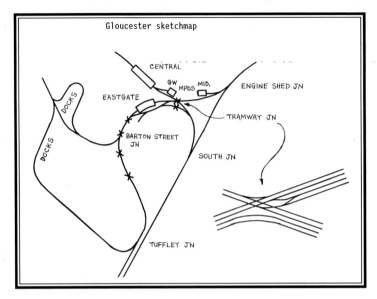

Gloucester sketchmap

John Corbett — the same who used his profits to turn the Welsh village of Towyn into a seaside resort. South of Abbots Wood, as we rattle the gates of Pirton crossing, a pair of '5Xs' appears belting towards us through Croome Perry Wood: the northbound 'Devonian' going hard at the long haul away from the River Avon. Soon it is our turn to face an adverse grade again, but there is the welcome prospect of a stop soon, and as it happens we find the distant signal on at Cleeve and brake down to 20mph before we see the home come off. That was probably due to a delay in the varied and crowded traffic in Cheltenham.

Cheltenham has a thoroughly inconvenient layout of three stations and a complex junction at Lansdown where the Midland, Great Western and Midland & South Western Junction lines meet. Between two and three in the afternoon a lot happens. In the northbound direction the 1.52pm Gloucester-Birmingham stopping train calls at Lansdown station at 2.6pm. The 11.5am from Paddington runs through the junction at 2.15pm to terminate in St James, followed by the 9.40am MSWJ goods from Swindon, which passes at 2.17pm and enters High Street goods depot at 2.24pm. St James receives the 1.40pm from Kingham at 2.33pm and the 2.30pm railcar from Gloucester at 2.46pm. Southbound, the 7.30am Newcastle-Bristol, which has travelled via Worcester, calls at Lansdown from 2.11pm to 2.16pm, the 8.15am Newcastle-Cardiff from 2.19pm

to 2.24pm, and the 'Devonian' from 2.29pm to 2.34pm. At 2.30pm a GW rail motor leaves St James, reverses at Malvern Road and heads off to Honeybourne. At 2.35pm an engine which brought in the 10.10am goods from Southampton leaves Alstone sidings light, reverses at Lansdown Junction and goes into St James. At 2.40pm a local to Gloucester departs from St James. It is not surprising that we were checked.

As soon as we stop in Lansdown station we put the engine in mid gear, open the cylinder cocks and apply the steam brake using its independent handle. The fireman opens both dampers, takes from a tool box a very non-steam-age tool — an electric torch — and squeezes down between the engine and the platform with a view to trying whether he can see the state of the ashpan. The driver walks along to the front end to look at the smokebox door. It is tight, but as he turns back he at once sees the cause of our difficulty. The elbow entering the smokebox from the brake ejector is loose; in fact it is not fixed at all. Someone must have neglected to tighten the bolts and they have fallen out. (Don't lambast the fitters, there was a problem over protective gear to get in the smokebox.) Through this hole is being drawn air that should go through the fire, resulting in lack of draught and lack of steam. There is nothing to be done about it now, as she would have to cool down for several hours before anyone could enter the smokebox to refit it. At this point we are interrupted

Right:
The 1 in 69 climb from Bristol to the north was one where banking engines were provided. Class 2 2-6-2T No 41240 has banked the 'Cornishman' on 7 April 1958, and is dropping back as the train passes Fishponds station. The notice by the buffer stop is a Midland one; we cannot understand the pettiness of a government that takes such trouble to paint out small reminders of the old companies. *Ivo Peters*

Right:
On 3 May 1958 the down 'Cornishman' was routed over the Midland and is seen approaching Mangotsfield behind ex-GWR 'Castle' class No 5045 *Earl of Dudley*. The chocolate and cream BR Standard set is augmented by a GWR Hawksworth in the new maroon livery. *Ivo Peters*

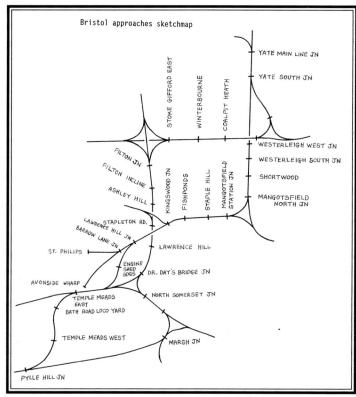

Bristol approaches sketchmap

YATE MAIN LINE JN
YATE SOUTH JN
STOKE GIFFORD EAST
WINTERBOURNE
COALPIT HEATH
FILTON JN
WESTERLEIGH WEST JN
FILTON INCLINE
WESTERLEIGH SOUTH JN
ASHLEY HILL
KINGSWOOD JN
FISHPONDS
STAPLE HILL
MANGOTSFIELD STATION JN
SHORTWOOD
MANGOTSFIELD NORTH JN
STAPLETON RD.
LAWRENCE HILL JN
BARROW LANE JN
LAWRENCE HILL
ST. PHILIPS
ENGINE SHED SDGS
DR. DAY'S BRIDGE JN
AVONSIDE WHARF
TEMPLE MEADS EAST
BATH ROAD LOCO YARD
NORTH SOMERSET JN
TEMPLE MEADS WEST
MARSH JN
PYLLE HILL JN

Above:
A Midland train sent via the GW route: No 45301 with an up extra passing through the yards at Stoke Gifford East on 10 August 1963. On the skyline is a building of the Bristol Aeroplane factory at Filton. *D. J. Wall*

Right:
Temple Meads 1: the old station — not Brunel's but the end-on extension. BR Standard Class 3 2-6-2T No 82041 in Platform 14 with the 12.50pm to Bath on 3 October 1964. A diesel train on the right is presumably due out first. This engine appears to have had a speedometer which has been removed. *B. J. Ashworth*

by the guard, who wants us to draw up as the rear part of the train is off the inadequate platform. Hastily retrieving our fireman, we set the engine in motion until we get a red flag and three blasts on the guard's whistle. At the same time a conference brings a decision that, having got so far, we will probably be able to take her through, so when finally signalled off we get away at 2.38pm.

The congested section from Cheltenham to Gloucester was quadrupled during the war. This area saw much activity then, as it is connected with the martial industry of aviation; two miles out of Cheltenham we see over to our right Staverton airfield, where the first British jet aircraft flew, and on its far side the Dowty factory (the same firm uses the restored Midland warehouse at Ashchurch and is the major employer in these parts). Other related industries include Quedgeley Air Ministry Stores and the Hoffman ball-bearing factory at Stonehouse. It is only a 10min run to Gloucester, and with a full glass to start with we manage it on the reserve in the boiler. Three pairs of signals face us as we pull out alongside the GW line, the left for the MSWJ, the middle for the down relief line and the right for the down main, which is for us — the main lines are the middle pair of the four. The arms are something foreign to Midland eyes, Great Western lower quadrant signals used as far as Churchdown where they revert to LMS upper quadrants. We run on the down main as far as Engine Shed Junction where, slowing to 35mph, we turn right on to the Barnwood curve past the Midland engine shed.

The layout at Gloucester was originally two terminal stations, the Midland one lying to the south of the GW one. They were replaced by the present Eastgate and Central respectively. At the point where the two routes crossed on the level they crossed a third early railway, the narrow-gauge Cheltenham & Gloucester, which gave the intersection its name of Tramway Junction; the latter is now a road. The Barnwood curve also has four tracks, the outer two connecting into the GW South curve for direct access between Cheltenham and Central. This is where we part company with the Newcastle-Cardiff train, which goes into Central. All Midland

route trains go through Eastgate, which dates only from 1896, built on what was originally a branch to the extensive dock area. The docks are still an important traffic source and 44 companies have railway facilities there. South of Tuffley Junction are four tracks, but they are worked as two double lines.

Eastgate has only three platforms; as we run in the up line is occupied by the 11.37am Bournemouth-Derby through train and the other down line is set for the 2.40pm from Cheltenham which has been following us block for block. We will pay a social call on our colleagues on *Kempenfelt*, to thank them for their co-operative attitude. They have got one hell of a fire in her and she is blowing-off heartily, prepared to push us to Bristol if necessary. They are confident of getting through without loss of time, but just in case, we agree that, if given the tip, our colleague will open his vacuum ejector. That is quite unofficial and there will be no need to mention it to anyone else. Returning to our footplate where we left the injector and blower on, we knock the former off and shut the doors. Smart station work has us away only two minutes late and with a majestic roll of man-made thunder we lift the train out beneath the overhead signalbox at Barton Street level crossing. An ascent at 1 in 108 follows, over three more crossings. As expected, this pulls her back to 200lb again and it is a constant balancing act, text-book firing to find an optimum thickness over every part of the grate, setting the injector to recover the water level here or sacrifice a little there, choosing a regulator opening and cut-off that will give more than normal exhaust blast to offset the loss through the hole but not use more steam than the boiler is producing. In this way we carry on, just about holding our own and, thanks to the well audible efforts from behind, keeping time. Indeed, no one on the train would know that anything is amiss.

At Standish Junction the GW lines bear away to the left on their climb into the Cotswold Hills. We keep straight on past Stonehouse Bristol Road, where the Nailsworth branch has a separate platform tucked away under the trees, and a 50mph speed limit gives us, in this situation, a welcome respite. The stations along here all had delightful Brunel chalet buildings, which have been more or less mutilated, and stone goods sheds with little wagon

turntables of which some remain. The line keeps to the low-lying Severn lands, until after Berkeley Road South it turns inland towards the North Somerset coalfield, subjecting us to a long bank to a summit at Rangeworthy. This proves a severe test to our engine; although we give it a good try, eventually with pressure back to 175lb the fire just won't burn any faster and we have to start easing her back. She completes the climb on first valve and 20%. As agreed, the quietening in *Leander's* voice is the signal for a surge of power from behind. Clear, crisp and pure, the 'Jubilee' note rings across the fields, tearing through Wickwar's peaceful village station and into 1,400yd Wickwar Tunnel, where it drums in our ears until the whole confined space is humming in sympathy. The schedule demands an average of 59mph up here, about the hardest part of the run, and there is no other way even with a good engine than to pile the black diamonds in and thrash her. However, we still have the tractive force available from six cylinders to give us fast acceleration from Gloucester and the Frocester slack, and the schedule contains 10min 'recovery time' on the last leg into Bristol. If we can just keep it together for a few more minutes we will be home. Firefly-like sparks are now arcing from *Kempenfelt's* chimney and a column of smoke is going straight up for five feet before it spreads out, to the accompaniment of a rock-solid six to the bar beat that makes our whistle seem almost superfluous. Over the top and our fireman whangs the doors open in a final abandon, shovels a good pile of coal in the back of the box, shuts everything including the tender front doors, and flops on to his seat. A grin and nod are exchanged across the footplate. He turns to look out of the front as we approach Yate and its junctions.

Two routes are available from Yate to Bristol, the Midland line via Mangotsfield or a link line up from a flyover junction at Yate to the GW Badminton-South Wales line and a left turn at Stoke Gifford. The up 'Devonian' takes the latter route, whereas the Western's 'Cornishman' to Birmingham takes the Midland route, an arrangement which keeps the crews on both sides familiar with both routes. Gathering speed we are soon whistling through the shunting at Westerleigh marshalling yards, and keep the pace up until the massive buildings of Carson's mills come into sight. Our col-

Right:

Temple Meads 2: the 1870 overall roof. This was on the occasion of the 1954 revival of the 'Bristolian', when 'King' class No 6000 *King George V*, identified by her bell, worked the first turn.
P. Winding

Right:

Temple Meads 3: the 1935 platforms. The 8.22am from Witham, via the Cheddar Valley, is pictured in Platform 6 after arrival on 28 September 1959.
M. Mensing

Below:

The western approach to Temple Meads and Bath Road bridge: the Manchester-Penzance through train stands in Platform 5. *C. R. L. Coles*

league has shut off and the show is once more ours, so we pull the brake handle down to destroy about 7in of vacuum and hold it until the brakes are on right down the train, then put it back to Running so that we are down to 30mph as she takes the junction curve and coasts on through Mangotsfield station. It is now 3.32pm, so we have 12min to cover the five miles down to Bristol, our destination spread out before us from this windy location on the side of Rodway Hill. The only problem left is keeping the fire lively enough to hold pressure up for the brakes, and that is accomplished by gradually levelling it down and keeping the blower on. We cruise through Staple Hill Tunnel and emerge into the built-up area, and exchange greetings with the 3.35pm Bristol-Bournemouth service, a train which goes straight on at Mangotsfield to Bath Green Park, and thence over the Somerset & Dorset. Inevitably, the signals are on at Lawrence Hill; we are following an empty stock working from the sidings here into Temple Meads. This stock forms the 4.15pm departure to Gloucester, and there is no point in trying to sneak in early. We have to draw steam on her again round past our home base, Barrow Road locomotive depot, and finally come to a stand facing the Great Western junction to watch a railcar trundling in on a local working from Severn Beach. On our right a Class 5 shouts past with more empty coaches, the stock of the 9.20am through train from York on its way out to Lawrence Hill. They hold us for less than a minute, then we get the road across the layout at Temple Meads East; instead of going into the great overall roof we are put over to the left in Platform 1. The Local Instructions state that the station must be treated as a terminus, so we roll gently in ready to stop all the way until bringing her to a stand at the far end above the river.

Bristol to Newton Abbot

Bristol, home of the Society of Merchant Venturers, has looked outward since before John Cabot sailed with the first properly organised expedition to the New World in 1497. Any ship that would withstand the tides and rocks of the Bristol Channel had to be exceptionally strong, especially about the bottom; the toughest ships in the world were built in Bristol fashion. Isambard Kingdom Brunel's *Great Western* and *Great Britain* were built here and modern firms such as Elder Dempster and Elders & Fyffes operate from new facilities at Avonmouth. Messrs Stothert & Slaughter began building railway engines here in 1837, and Fox, Walker & Co in 1863. They amalgamated and took over the Avonside Ironworks to form the Avonside Engine Co. Avonside was, in turn, taken over by Hunslet in 1934. Fox Walker's Atlas Locomotive Works were acquired by Peckett. Largely as a result of the efforts of these two firms, more railway engines were built in Bristol than in Derby. The Bristol Wagon & Carriage Works turned out factory-built horse-drawn vehicles and invented the railway container. The Douglas Brothers began making motor-cycles in 1883. The Bristol Tramways & Carriage Co used its workshops to build the first British production aircraft to be ordered by the Army, and began building motorbuses and lorries in 1913. Both those enterprises became market leaders in their own fields. The Bristol Aeroplane Co took over Brazil-Straker & Co, aero-engine specialists founded in 1917, and its achievements include the turbo-prop engine in 1945 and the first British helicopter in 1947. For a while after the war it also built motor-cars. Now it is developing two more advanced concepts: the Pegasus vertical take-off jet engine and the Bristol 198 supersonic transport aircraft. In short, every kind of conveyance has been developed and manufactured here, and in the breadth of its contribution to progress in transport, Bristol is unique.

Its first railway was built to bring coal from mines in the area of Coalpit Heath down to the River Avon. This was called the Bristol & Gloucestershire Railway and opened on 6 August 1835. This is basically the route down which we have just come with the 'Devonian'. When it was incorporated into the larger Bristol & Gloucester in 1844 it was rebuilt to broad gauge, and was unusual in being worked by the contractor who supplied its rolling stock, Stothert & Slaughter. They started their brief tenure by derailing the inaugural train. When the Midland took it over they added a third rail and brought their first standard gauge trains through in 1854. And of course we have the Great Western Railway, founded at a meeting in Bristol Guildhall on 30 July 1833 and opened from here to Bath on 31 August 1840.

Bristol Temple Meads station is situated where the Great Western and its contemporary the Bristol & Exeter met at right angles, and the resultant curved configuration is similar to another great station, York. Brunel's original terminus lies on the north side, and is still used, appropriately by trains on the earliest route, the Gloucester line. The station was extensively reconstructed and enlarged between 1931 and 1935 in a programme which included quadrupling the main line from Filton, a new carriage depot at Malago Vale, new stations at Bedminster and Parson Street, resignalling with colour light signals, huge signalboxes at Temple Meads East and West with their aggressively avant-garde styling, and new platforms, Nos 1-5, outside the main roof. The longest platform, Nos 9/10, is 1,363ft in length. The entire station is built on arches over the low-lying ground by the Floating Harbour, which is the former River Avon converted into a basin by William Jessop in the early 19th century. To the north, Temple Meads goods is the world's largest covered goods station and contrasts with the original B & G terminus at Avonside Wharf on the other side of the water. To the south is Bath Road locomotive depot, site of the Bristol & Exeter's original workshops.

In the Running Foreman's office at the depot, a short discussion has taken place, as the load for the 'Devonian' has been wired through and, at 445 tons, is over the limit of 420 tons for a 'Hall' class engine from Bristol. The driver agrees to take it, provided that the overload is noted and will excuse him for any loss of time, and that he is given an assisting engine from Taunton at least as far as Whiteball Tunnel. He then goes out to rejoin his engine: on this occasion they have borrowed one from Taunton shed, No 4920 *Dumbleton Hall*. She was one of the first batch of 'Halls' built at Swindon in 1929, but more important than her age is the fact that she received a Heavy General Overhaul in January, thus meeting the first criterion of those of us who are going to ride her on a fast train — no axlebox knocks. Coincidentally, we passed the actual Dumbleton Hall earlier today; it lies five miles east of Ashchurch.

On being given the news that he has been volunteered to boil more water than the stipulated maximum, the fireman makes the usual reply and continues his occupation of laying down a fire of hand-picked and thrown lumps. A piece of good Welsh coal will swell and open up like a flower when it is heated, and having little volatile content will burn slowly and steadily, so by the time we have to leave we will have a box-full, hot all through almost like a bed of coke. The engine is well cleaned up, and what a pleasure it is to see her in true green after the killjoy black imposed by the Railway Executive in their desire for change. At 3.40pm we phone up Bath Road Loco Yard signalbox and he pulls off the shed signal for us to run out over the bridge. The 'Devonian' pulls in alongside. With *Leander's* cab swept down and her crew looking over the side, faces washed and ties straight, from the platform side she presents a perfectly normal appearance, although on our side we can see an area of burnt-off paint around the ejector exhaust elbow. The two 'Jubilees' are uncoupled and run forward down the engine line towards Bath Road bridge, then we pull forward over a slip crossing and back on. The 'Hall' looks markedly slimmer than the engines she has

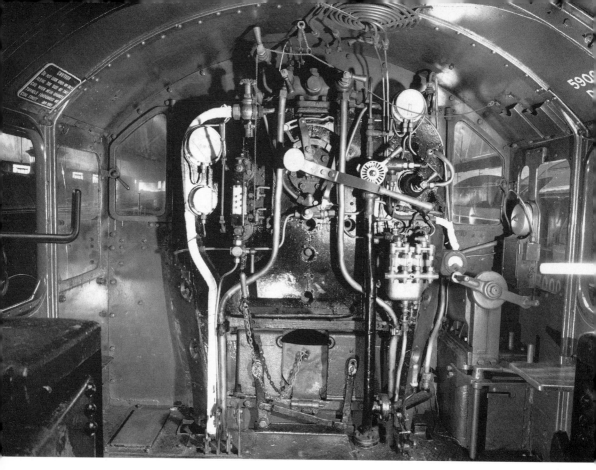

Above:
The interior of a 'Hall' class cab; the brake controls are in the 'Off' position and the regulator is open. On the extreme left is the tender handbrake handle, and on the right the bright object is the water-scoop handle reflecting the photography lights. This is No 5900 *Hinderton Hall*, which does not have an exhaust steam injector, hence the middle stop valve on the turret is blanked off. The exhaust injector is an economy device in that it transfers heat from the exhaust to the feed water, but on the average preserved engine, whose injectors are used mostly when the regulator is closed, it confers little benefit. These GW footplate views were taken by kind permission of the Great Western Society at Didcot.
C. J. Austin

Left:
The driver's controls on No 6998 *Burton Agnes Hall.* Here the brake is 'On' and the regulator is shut, so that its jockey arm has lowered the curved slotted link, shutting off steam from the valve below that blows oil into the cylinders. *C. J. Austin*

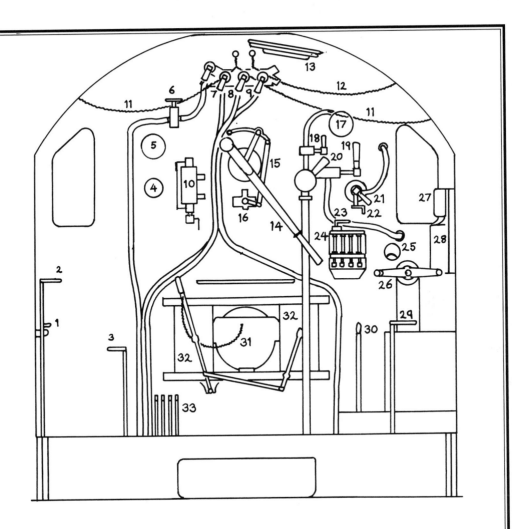

Cab Controls, Hall Class Engine

1	Hose-pipe cock	17	Vacuum Gauge
2	Exhaust injector water regulator	18	Small ejector steam
3	Exhaust injector cone adjust	19	Large ejector steam
4	Train heat gauge	20	Brake application valve
5	Boiler pressure gauge	21	Blower
6	Train heat valve	22	Lubricator warming cock
7	Exhaust injector live steam	23	Lubricator water cock
8	Exhaust injector supplementary steam	24	Hydrostatic lubricator
		25	Speedometer (if fitted)
9	Live injector steam	26	Reverser
10	Boiler water gauge	27	ATC bell
11	Whistle pull	28	ATC control box
12	Alarm whistle pull	29	Gravity sand handles
13	Lubricator condenser coil	30	Cylinder cocks
14	Regulator	31	Firedoor flap
15	Regulator jockey arm	32	Firedoors
16	Atomiser steam valve	33	Dampers

replaced, but comparison of the dimensions shows that she is much of a size with them. The visual effect is due mainly to the height of the chimney and safety valve bonnet, for she is seven inches taller than they are and these fittings have a disproportionate influence on the impression we gain of the engine. The most obvious difference is the lack of valve motion on the outside. The 'Hall' has Stephenson link motion installed between the frames, actuating the valves by rocking shafts. When preparing her it is necessary to go underneath, but you can stand up behind the driving axle to oil the eccentrics and ahead of the links to oil them, and it is far better than the four-cylinder 'Castle' in that respect. There are outside oiling points as well: the coupling and connecting rods, an oil box on the top slide bar, the crosshead and two corks on the valve rod have to be attended to. The other point of comparison, that there is only one of her, is due not to any innate superiority but to the road being easier from here on.

When we have coupled up we can take a look around the activity in the station. There are eight trains: in Platform 8 the 3.5pm diesel from Portishead; in Platform 11 another ready to depart at 3.50pm to Portishead; in Platform 3 the 2.11pm Exeter-Wolverhampton service with a 'Castle' due out at 3.52pm; in Platform 5 the Penzance-Wolverhampton 'Cornishman' express is, as yet, without an engine; in Platform 12 the 4.2pm to Severn Beach; in Platform 6 the 4.12pm to Taunton with another 'Hall'; in Platform 9 the 4.15pm to

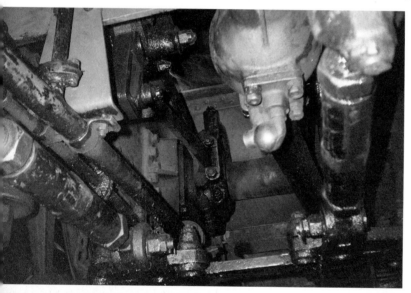

Left:
The valve motion on a 'Hall' is between the frames. This view up from below shows the right side expansion link and eccentrics. The bulbous object is an oil separator in the pipe supplying steam to the exhaust injector. On either side are brake pull rods. *SHA*

Left:
The main frames of a 'Hall' extend only as far as the cylinders. Looking up past the bogie frame, the end of a bar which carries the front buffer beam can be seen bolted to the back of the cylinder block. Later-build 'Halls' have conventional full-length frames which can be seen projecting above the front platform. *SHA*

Paddington with a 'King'; and in Platform 13 the 4.15pm to Gloucester with a Standard 2-6-2T.

At 4pm the guard pushes a signal plunger to indicate that we are ready to start, and the signal turns green. The driver puts her in full forward gear, opens the regulator slightly and waits while steam roars from the cylinder cocks. *Dumbleton Hall* seems to pause and think about it, then she moves off with a sudden explosive bark, another, a spit from the crosshead vacuum pump, and more of the same. Crossing over to the down main and under Bath Road bridge the beat is coming out sharp and clear, still in full gear, which on these engines means a cut-off of nearly 90%, giving an even torque on the wheels that is the secret of their ability to keep

their feet when lifting heavy loads. Round the curve at Pylle Hill goods yard, we pass the two '5Xs', waiting for a path back through the station, their crews putting away some much-needed tea. In the traditional manner we pull the fire through with the long pricker, sliding it through the closed doors, then as the driver winds the reverser back a notch or two, open the doors and put the flap up. Steadily, for there is no doubt she has a big load behind her, *Dumbleton Hall* starts to work up speed.

On the climb out of Bristol we cannot expect much in the way of speed, so when she is up to about 45mph we link her up until the blast is but a bass accompaniment to the air-pump spits — the speed is a matter of feel, for these engines do not

Right:
Connecting trains are seen at Yatton in the 1960s: on the left, a diesel car on the Clevedon shuttle; 'Hall' No 4947 *Nanhoran Hall* on a Bristol-Weston stopper; 2-6-2T No 41249 on a Cheddar Valley line train. *R. E. Toop*

Below:
Puxton & Worle station was near neither of those villages and all that remained of it by 1961 was the main building. No 4949 *Packwood Hall* passes the closed station on 6 August that year. The headlamps show that the train is the empty stock of a summer extra, returning from Weston-super-Mare. *M. J. Fox*

have speedometers. It is now time to start firing. The GW firehole flap almost closes the hole and must be pulled down using the chain provided. It lies just past the vertical when up, and of course the pull of the blast holds it in place. One soon acquires the flick of the chain to lift it up. The fire is actually well above the firehole rim at each side, where the fireman adds several shovelfuls at each round, with a lower saddle in the middle over which he makes four shots down the front to finish before putting the flap up again. It is some minutes before the water comes into sight below the top of the gauge-glass, then he starts the exhaust injector and fiddles it to the minimum feed rate he can obtain. The driver opens her out to full regulator and 25% cut-off.

The summit is marked by a short 110yd tunnel in a long cutting, after which a view opens out ahead as we rush through Flax Bourton station. The fireman takes a breather, to wave to a colleague on a pannier tank shunting out the Ministry of Fuel's Tyntesfield branch, but he has to resume shovelling almost at once because his mate has not eased her as he usually does and she charges down into the Somerset moors.

A moor is a tract of flat land; it does not have to be high up, and these are only about 15ft above mean sea level. Now largely drained, they are the richest dairy country in England, but they were peat bogs, and towns like Yatton were sited on low islands. As we fly through Yatton, going pretty well now, the rail motor that runs the shuttle to Clevedon is in the up side bay, and there passes the other way an ex-GWR 2-8-0 hauling the 10.50am Hackney Yard-Avonmouth goods working. There is also a pannier tank in the goods yard, standing pilot for the afternoon before working the 6.13pm Cheddar Valley line passenger train to Frome. Another couple of miles and we are up to 70mph and the floor is not keeping very good contact with our feet, but soon we must think about slowing to 20mph for Worle Junction, where we turn off the main line to go into Weston-super-Mare. We have taken one minute over the scheduled time.

When the railway opened, Weston was a minor resort and fishing port, served by a branch line from where White House Farm is now, past the gas works to what is now the goods station, and whose 'train' was a horse-drawn coach. Sunny and sheltered between Worlebury Hill and Brean Down, all it lacks is the sea, for the water of the Bristol Channel recedes a mile and a half at low tide, leaving nothing in sight except brown sand. For all that, it became popular with people from Bristol and the Midlands, and it is a favourite resort for the Swindon Works holiday. The masses are catered for by Locking Road excursion platforms. Today we pull into the main station, past the 4.35pm to London which is making its final preparations, with our blower hard on. That is not because she is shy for steam, but to keep the thick bed of Welsh coal alive. Three minutes later, the safety valves start to blow, not with the explosion of a 'pop' valve but with a steady hissing that does not drown the sound of the guard's whistle. We start her up carefully and again, sure-footed, she moves off steadily if rather slowly. Regaining the main line at Uphill Junction, we settle down to some hard pulling. Ahead to our left the skyline is dominated by 460ft Brent Knoll, but everything else is flatness.

Highbridge is a decayed port, once important enough to be the terminus of the Somerset & Dorset Joint Railway, but it has not seen a ship these 10 years. The S&D crosses the main line on the level just north of the station, with a curious little wedge-shaped signalbox. Bridgwater is another port which has seen better days, although in this case the dock branch is still in business. It crosses the Bristol and Bath roads in the town centre and has an opening bridge over the River Parrett. Some modern industries have also moved in to continue the traditional trades; Clark's shoes, Van Heusen shirts and British Cellophane are among the firms working here. A lot of trains call, including the 2.50pm Stoke Gifford-Tavistock Junction express goods, which is ahead of us and which we have been overhauling all the way from Bristol. It should be inside the down goods loop by the time we reach Dunball. Here the driver shuts down to drifting steam, none too soon for he has clearly been mortgaging the boiler. Pressure is down to 200lb with only half a glass of water. However, we are still on time, having averaged just over 40mph start to stop.

Besides the goods train, we may also glimpse an unusual engine, little ex-Cardiff Railway tank No 1338. Her job is to shunt Bridgwater and Dunball wharf sidings, running daily from her home base at Taunton.

From the platform end at Weston-super-Mare, '5X' No 45725 *Repulse*, with a freshly made-up fire and too much steam, is ready to start from Locking Road station with the 12.15pm to Sheffield. It is August 1962; the train number 1E68 is the BR equivalent of the numbering system invented by the Great Western. The signal is the up bay platform starter.
G. F. Heiron

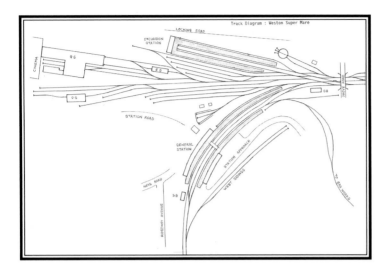

Track Diagram : Weston Super Mare

Below:
A through train, formed of LMS coaches with a GW engine, heads for Bristol from Cogload Junction. A generous helping of coal has just been placed on the fire. On the left is the down line incline to a bridge over the London line in the distance.
J. G. Hubback

A mile south of Bridgwater we cross an ordinary-looking overslung Warren girder bridge over the River Parrett; this was the Brunel bridge nobody heard about, the one that didn't work. It was built as a brick arch like Maidenhead but with only half the rise, but shifting of the piers, not surprising when you look around at the acres of mud, sedges and wet fields, proved too much for the brickwork and it was quietly replaced by an iron span. The original abutments remain. Here we again flog the engine up to about a mile a minute, which takes us as far as Durston and knocks her well back. The fireman is plying shovel and flap-plate almost continuously, firing all over the grate with the back now level and white-hot. Mostly he is putting on dust, for Welsh coal tends to pulverise easily and

ends up as large lumps in a quantity of soft slack. Approaching Cogload flyover the driver winds her into 50% and slams the regulator full open, and the chimney sounds like a machine gun. Any tendency for the fire to settle and clinker-up will certainly have been cured now. The engine gallops up the incline to cross over the main line from Reading on the bridge built in 1934 when the junction was rearranged and the line from here to Norton Fitzwarren quadrupled. Beyond, the down road from Bristol becomes the relief, so *Dumbleton Hall* is shut off and a brake application steadies her down to take a high speed crossover on to the main. The fireman uses the coal-pick and short pricker to pull some coal forward in the tender and select out some lumps, with which he starts

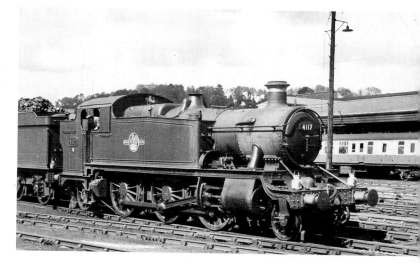

Right:
The 2-6-2T which banks us up to Whiteball, No 4117, is smartly turned out in green livery and carrying express passenger headlights, possibly in readiness for just such a job. *R. C. Riley*

Right:
At Newton Abbot on 9 June 1960, the crew of 2-6-2T No 4145 prepares its engine. The driver swings a water crane over while the fireman climbs on top to open the tank filler. Note an oil feeder on the side gangway and an oil can on the front. In the background is a cooling tower of Newton Abbot power station. *Ian Allan Library*

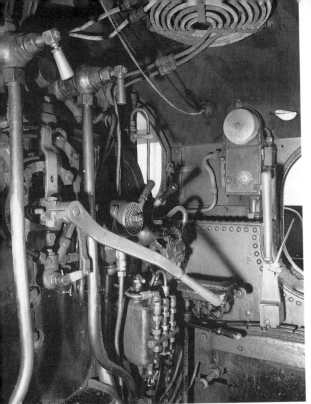

Above left:
In a 2-6-2T cab, driver's side: to the right is the reversing lever, set in a forward gear position; above it, the ATC box has an additional feature, a window labelled 'Shoe Catch'. This is engine No 6106, whose ATC shoe can be raised and locked up when running on London area electrified lines. *C. J. Austin*

Above:
The fireman's side on No 6106; a firing shovel is leaning against the back end of the water tank, in front of an inspection hatch. A water gauge sits on top of the tank. *C. J. Austin*

Centre left:
A demonstration of how much room you have to swing a shovel on a Great Western tank engine. *C. J. Austin*

Below left:
The rear axle on 2-6-2T No 6106, showing the axleboxes sliding in their curved housing. *SHA*

Above:
**Typifying the Great Western holiday train, the
9.30am Paddington-Newquay service of
27 July 1953 comes out of Whiteball Tunnel
and races down the bank, alongside a running
goods loop which extends to Burlescombe.
The engine is No 6007** *King William III.*
J. G. Hubback

Below:
**In the Devon sunshine on 9 August 1956,
No 4991** *Cobham Hall* **pulls away from Dawlish
Warren through Langstone Rock. The railway
was originally built where the footpath is now.
Some of the original broad gauge rail is still
here, forming a post at the near end of the
wall.** *T. E. Williams*

Above:
This view of 2-6-2T No 4157 taking 12 coaches away from Dawlish Warren makes you wonder why anyone needed tender engines at all. It also shows the vast amount of rock tipped to protect the railway, and the Warren itself, from the sea. *R. J. Blenkinsop*

Below:
An undated, probably early 1950s, view from Langstone towards Dawlish, with a 'Castle', possibly No 5028 *Llantilio Castle*, on an up train. By the tail of the train is the notorious Sea Lawn Gap.
Ian Allan Library

building up a fire again, working leisurely now. He pauses to turn to the right-hand side of the tender front and lower the scoop into Creech trough. He is anticipating coming off the train at Taunton to attach a second engine for assistance, and time saved on watering will be worthwhile. At this point two up trains pass almost simultaneously: the 3.42pm Exeter-Bristol service and a pannier tank chuffing importantly along with the 5pm stopper from Taunton to Frome. At Bathpool Mills the driver turns the blower on, shuts off and makes a single long brake application. He lets her roll for a bit, then makes another; the hiss of air into the brake valve is interrupted by a howl from the ATC siren, which he instantly stops by raising a small handle on the control box. Taunton East distant is on, but the warning was unnecessary as we have the train well under control. Almost all trains stop at Taunton, the county town of Somerset.

At the west end of Taunton station, in a siding outside the engine shed, a crew are watering and checking round their engine preparatory to banking the 'Devonian' to Whiteball. They have '5101' class 2-6-2T No 4117. She was built in 1936 at Swindon and has worked in this area all her life. This year she has led a shuttlecock existence, as from Taunton she was transferred to Exeter in March, but was moved back to Taunton in June for the summer season, principally to augment the local

strength on this banking job. At 5pm the driver appears from the station where he has confirmed that their services will be required, so his mate makes up the fire. In the cramped cab space it is a great deal easier to swing a shovel when standing still than when the engine is bouncing about, so he intends to cram as much into the box as he can before starting.

Usual practice is to bank trains from Wellington, in which case the banker need not be coupled up, but when assisting through from Taunton, rules dictate that the banker must be coupled to the train. Fortunately the larger 2-6-2T classes may be put in front of the train engine, unless the latter is a 'King', on this section, which saves a lot of time. Knowing the routine, at 5.5pm our driver whistles up and moves forward. We are signalled out on to the down relief and stop there while the fireman crosses to Taunton West Station box to make sure the signalman knows we are there and what we are there for. By the time he returns the train is drawing up in Platform 5 with the engine beside the box, and there is no time to add any more coal before we get the road to move on to the front. No 4920's fireman takes advantage of not having to shunt to top up his tank, while her driver shuts off his ejector and destroys the vacuum, then goes round his engine feeling the big-ends and oiling the slidebars, so we are left to couple up and create the brake. Station business is fin-

Right:
Dawlish station, west end, looking over the low Colonnade Viaduct. No 4968 *Shotton Hall* is running in with a Paignton-Exeter stopper. *J. Davenport*

ished within the five minutes laid down, but the guard does not wave us away because he can see that the starting signal is still on. We have to inform the driver of the 'Hall' that we are assisting him as far as Burlescombe. We board our respective footplates, and now the starter comes off and we get the green flag. A tug on the whistle chain, echoed from behind, and we are off.

These tank engines also date from the period of intensive development at Swindon at the beginning of the century, and have undergone little change since then other than the addition of super-heaters. The wheel arrangement is different from that of the 2-6-2T we were on earlier in that the small carrying wheels under the cab are borne in the main frames. The bodies of the axleboxes are curved, forming arcs of a circle as viewed from above, and slide in curved guides under spring control so that the entire axle can traverse on a circular path. The pivoting truck carrying the front wheels is linked by compensating levers to the leading coupled axle, producing an engine that is quite capable of running at express speeds. And the boiler is similar to that on the record-breaking 'City' class express engines.

On the westward exit from Taunton we pass the west end junction of goods lines which avoid the passenger station, then Fairwater yard on the left. Over Silk Mill level crossing, on the right is a War Department depot served by Blinkhorn Sidings. Another mile and a half takes us to Norton Fitzwarren, a complex junction where the four tracks split into three double lines, to Exeter, Barnstaple and Minehead. This is the trouble spot on summer Saturdays, when extra trains to and from the North Devon resorts have to be funnelled through the Taunton bottleneck, and it is not unusual to take half an hour to get through. The line ahead is also critical, with the two streams of traffic from London and the Midlands constricted to one track on the climb over Whiteball, and many are the bored holidaymakers who, finding their train stopping and starting and getting down to Exeter an hour or two late, have looked out at the empty open roads and vowed to take to their own transport.

No 4117's crew are in Taunton No 4 link and do not often get the chance to work an express train, so they are going to make the most of it. The fireman, mindful of the number of opportunities to bang his knuckles, is keeping an even fire and feeding the front by bringing his shovel on to the firehole rim and then shooting at the desired spot. The driver, wedged comfortably between the side tank and tool box, has the regulator opened well onto the main valve and has her going a good deal faster than she is accustomed. He waves with satisfaction to one of his contemporaries on a '43xx' 2-6-0, coming slowly over the points at Norton Fitzwarren with the afternoon goods from Minehead. Just to be on the safe side he shuts off before pulling up the reverser, because handling a lever reverse on a big engine at speed is not easy and takes a lot of strength. He then opens up again and busies himself with a length of cord, which loops round the regulator handle and hitches over the body of the vacuum gauge. If he did but know it, the men behind, listening to the roar from the tank engine, are taking it quietly with their horse reined in to 25% and a steady firing rate. They are hoping not to have to draw any more coal forward before Exeter. It is difficult to assess our speed, but we pass Wellington 7½min after Norton, which is an average of 41mph, so we could well have reached 60mph. The gradient is really felt now, the regulator is hard on the stop and the exhaust really tearing from the chimney. She is maintaining full pressure against the injector, and the only question is whether the fireman can feed the fire fast enough. He makes such a determined attempt at this that his mate has to clap him on the shoulder and remind him that he is not going to Plymouth.

What a pleasure it is to be away from the levels, following the River Tone up to Poole Siding, through Wellington and into a narrow valley by West Ford. No 4920's driver condescends to open up to full regulator. At about 35mph the wonderfully crisp Swindon beat is heard in duet as the two engines cross Beam Bridge below Sampford Arundel church on the left. No thought of steel mills now, the most industrious sight is a herd of cows on the line-side lane, on their way up to Marlands. Into a deep cutting and Whiteball Tunnel comes into view. It is a long one, 1,088yd; with two engines steaming hard — the gradient is still up at 1 in 127 through it — the atmosphere will be a bit thick. No firing is done in the last half-mile so as to avoid

Right:
Looking down from above Kennaway Tunnel; the 'Castle' has emerged from Coryton Tunnel beside secluded Coryton Cove. On the down side is a GWR illuminated 40mph speed limit sign. *A. R. Butcher*

Below:
At the classic location of Parson's Tunnel, a down goods train hauled by one of the long-range 2-8-2Ts, No 7220. *E. D. Bruton*

smoke. Inside it is hot and choking, for a freight train has been through a few minutes before. Both men on No 4117 tie handkerchiefs over their faces and sit on the floor, leaving the engine to plug away unattended. That is the reason for the piece of string, otherwise the regulator would vibrate shut. After a minute and a half the fog becomes a little lighter. That is the sign to unhitch the string and start up the second injector, and as we emerge into daylight the fireman checks the gauge-glass, for running on to a down-grade and shutting the regulator causes boiler water level to fall by some four inches at the rear end. Both engines are cut down to drifting steam.

Whiteball signalbox stands by the west end of the tunnel and is a new replacement for the structure which burned out last winter when the signalman upset his oil lamp. A short siding on the up side is occupied by another 2-6-2T banker, waiting for a return path to Wellington after pushing the freight train up. Three-quarters of a mile further on is Burlescombe, a little country station nestling below the village. It is the junction for a short branch

Below:
We had to include a shot of a Great Western 4-6-0 emerging from Parson's Tunnel. No 5028 *Llantilio Castle* is pictured on the down 'Devonian' during the summer of 1957.
D. J. Fish

that curves across the Grand Western Canal into Westleigh quarry. The signalman here knows that the 'Devonian' is stopping to put off the pilot, as he was told over the telephone by the regulator at Taunton, and also received a telegraph signal from Whiteball of two, pause, two on the bell immediately after the two beats for 'Train entering section'. The train stops rather short, as No 4117's driver is not very sure about how the brake will behave and gives it the lot at first. The fireman climbs off as the engine comes to a stand; there is no shunter here. He ducks under the buffers, unclips the vacuum hose couplings and parts the hoses. Then he unscrews the coupling and lifts it off the drawhook of the 'Hall'. He places the hose of No 4117 on its dummy coupling, steps out into the cess and waves to his driver, who crosses back to the right side, releases the brake and takes the engine away. No 4920's driver gets down as he is putting the front hose on, and they exchange courtesies while the signalman works No 4117 over the road. He puts her on the branch, as he has the 12 noon Penzance-Crewe express to pass before sending her back.

When we get the road, before starting we whistle up and receive a green flag from the guard, because our train is partly alongside the station platform. We are now some four minutes behind time, but it is

downhill all the way to Exeter. The 'Hall' is soon up to 70mph, at which rate the cab is a right circus ring; if you have the balance of a horseback juggler, the heat resistance of a fire-eater, the muscles of a strong-man, and the eye of a sharpshooter, you might be able to run *Dumbleton Hall* to time. The fireman makes it easier for himself by having a fire very thick at the back, what is sometimes called a haycock fire, and putting most of the coal on there, letting it shake itself down to the front.

Sampford Peverell halt has loops for the platforms, and here we overtake the freight that was preceding us. It is the 8.10am coal train from Bassaleg in the Ebbw valley to Tavistock Junction, hauled by an engine unique to the Great Western, a '72xx' class 2-8-2T. It has a long bunker holding six tons of coal, the same as our tender, enabling this tank engine to work long-distance jobs, and it will, therefore, have worked through from Severn Tunnel Junction. At Tiverton Junction more freight shunting is going on, a pannier tank having brought the 5.20pm up from Tiverton and now disposing it before returning light. At this point the regulator is nearly shut and speed is allowed to fall off slightly in deference to a 65mph limit over a sharp reverse curve. Even when running easily the driver does not pull her up to less than 25%, owing to the characteristics of the Stephenson valve gear. The valve which admits steam to the engine cylinder is driven to and fro by an eccentric, which is advanced relative to its crank so that when the driver shortens the valve travel the latter closes at an earlier point in the piston stroke, this point being the cut-off. To improve fast running, the eccentric is further advanced so that the valve begins to open while the piston is approaching the cylinder end on the previous stroke to give a preliminary build-up of pressure called lead steam. However, as the cut-off is shortened the lead increases, until at very short settings it begins to hinder the action of the engine, losing power and setting up a fore-and-aft shaking which may be felt back in the train. The best performance will therefore be obtained by keeping a longer cut-off and controlling the engine with the regulator; which has other implications, but that is probably enough to be thinking about for now, along with watching the signals, remembering where we are and keeping to the scheduled running times.

On the run down to Exeter we pass two up trains, the 1.20pm Penzance-Paddington express and the 3.55pm Plymouth-Swindon parcels. This brings us to Cowley Bridge Junction where the Southern line from Barnstaple comes in, and at 50mph we come round the long bend into a narrow part of the Exe valley. Goods lines diverge into the extensive Riverside sidings, which are busy at this time of day. Two trains bound for Tavistock Junction are in, the 2.40pm from Bristol and the 7.10am from Rogerstone (also on the Ebbw just outside Newport), and a local working from Alphington Mill on the Teign Valley line has just arrived. Three shunting engines are at work. Freight workings here, as elsewhere, are more complex than the passenger services, and we have not seen the last of them yet.

It is just 6.9pm and at last we are setting out for what our passengers have come to see — the Devon seaside. From our position at the south end of St David's the city of Exeter rises to our left, crowned with its cathedral. Close at hand the incline to Central climbs away past the back of West box, as steep as the Lickey but on a sharp curve, with a tunnel as well.

We start away over the Exe bridge, through a stretch of water meadows to St Thomas station, which is nearer the city centre than St David's but, by contrast, has had little improvement and is still largely the original Brunel station. Standing in the up platform is the first of the stream of summer evening trains from Torbay, the 4.33pm from Kingswear to Exeter. A waterway comes close alongside, the Exeter Canal, the oldest artificial navigation in the country. For a while we run in a flat expanse between higher ground lined with settlements on the right and a gradually evident glint of water on the left. Although the tender is full, the fireman lowers the scoop over Exminster trough so that it just grazes the surface and throws up a cloud of spray that will produce a rainbow for anyone who happens to notice. Between Exminster and Powderham is an unmanned level crossing which has a peculiar working instruction. It is the only land access to the Turf Hotel, and if there is a fire there the Fire Brigade have to telephone Exeter Control, who presumably will have the trains stopped while fire appliances hurtle down the drive. Here the line takes up position by the Exe estu-

Above:
The 8.45am Plymouth-Liverpool working of 10 June 1949 is seen on the sea wall, passing Sprey Point between Teignmouth and Parson's **Tunnel. The engine is 'Castle' No 7000** *Viscount Portal,* **then only some two years old. The hill in the background is Shaldon on the far side of the Teign.** *E. D. Bruton*

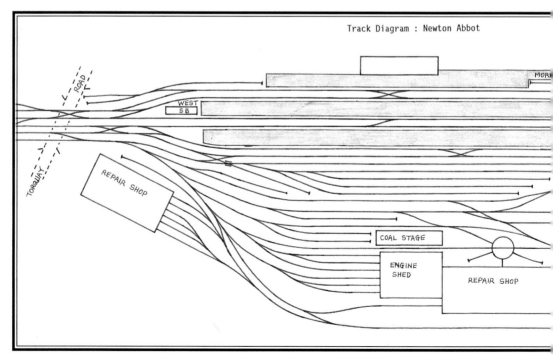

Track Diagram : Newton Abbot

ROAD

TORQUAY

WEST
S B

MOR

REPAIR SHOP

COAL STAGE

ENGINE
SHED

REPAIR SHOP

ary, a shining expanse beginning to insinuate that exciting salty tang into carriage windows. At Starcross little boats are lying all over the place. The resort of Exmouth lies on the far shore, with beyond it the nothingness which so fascinates the English that the most landlubberly of us will travel all this way just to have a glimpse of it. The driver slows down and takes the 45mph limit through Starcross a little fast, then adjusts the regulator to keep her going steady at that. By now the fireman has established a black mound inside the firehole. To avoid making too much smoke, every minute or so he pushes the top of it down with the shovel to reveal a bright surface on to which he fires fresh coal. In the event of pressure falling he pushes a couple down to the front.

Two non-passenger trains passed on this run are the 12.20pm Penzance-Kensington milk, a fast service worked by a 'Castle', and the 2.26pm goods from Tavistock Junction to Swindon. As we pass Dawlish Warren Halt on the through road, the 5.20pm from Paignton comes by. On the up side the old goods yard is now occupied by camping coaches, whose windows look across to where the Warren divides the estuary from the sea proper. The sun seems to become brighter, the air clearer, the breeze keener. The 'Hall' leans to a

curve in a great rock defile through the back of Langstone Cliff, then we are beside the open sea, sparkling in the evening sun.

This section is arguably the best-loved piece of railway in the country. Thanks to the energetic publicity department of the Great Western Railway, the image of red sandstone cliffs with a green engine on the sea wall above blue sea is the embodiment of summer to many of us. Of course we know it is not always blue; we know that the proximity of large amounts of salt water is a constant threat to the operation of signalling equipment and the civil engineers are always worrying about the security of the wall; we know about the winter storms when trains have to use the Southern route round to the north of Dartmoor. But civil engineers are not romantics; their only reaction to dramatic scenery is to want to alter it. This is not a place where commercial considerations should rule; this is a railway for happiness. If British Railways have any sense at all they will play it for all they are worth, put on extra trains, run observation coaches, open halts, reduce fares, advertise in every boarding house; here is where railways might shake off their dirty, worn, queue and ration image and shine out as a responsive community service enhancing

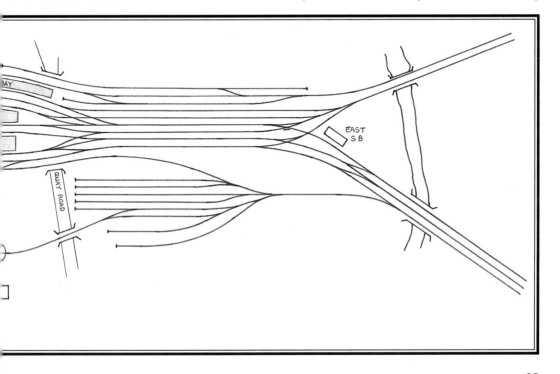

pleasure as well as profit, to the fore in every holidaymaker's memories of the one part of his life he wants to savour and recall.

We pull up in Dawlish station, literally on the beach in front of this most decorous resort, a place of neat window-boxes and quiet gardens where retired gentlefolk stroll in white flannels. From now on there is no demand for continuous steaming and in spite of the heavy load making the engine strive noisily to lift it from stops, we can give her some stick without fear of winding her. The fireman changes to his stopping-train mode of working; keeping the flap shut while starting away, firing during the run-up to speed, turning the injector on when the regulator is closed. In between spotting signals he washes up, tidies his bag and puts his tea-can away.

You can walk along the line from the Warren to Dawlish on the sea wall, except for a gap where the owners of Sea Lawn House would not allow the rude populace in sight of their windows and at high tide you have to cross a footbridge up to the main road. The south end of Dawlish stops abruptly at Lea Mount, through which the train goes in the 209yd Kennaway Tunnel. Next comes a stretch which we have to ourselves, for there is no public landward access; Coryton Cove, Coryton Tunnel (231yd), Horse Cove, Phillot Tunnel (55yd), Shell Cove, Clerk's Tunnel (66yd), Smugglers Cliff and Breeches Rock. We are heading straight into the sun and the coruscation off the sea obscures our view almost entirely. Then into sudden darkness

again, Parson's Tunnel, which in 1921 was built out at the north end to its present length of 512yd to provide shelter from rock falls. If you look back on emerging from the tunnel you will catch a glimpse of the Parson and Clerk, although these rocks have worn away so much within living memory that they have lost the shapes that gave them their names. This is the spot where the classic view of the Great Western holiday train was taken. There is a print of it in 'Cheltenham Flyer' of 1934 and it looks much the same today. From here to Teignmouth is another wall walk on which one may stroll free from the noise, dirt, litter and danger of a motor road which so often mars a sea-front. The driver is on the cliff side, and the fireman's job along here is one of public relations; a wave to a family party and a toot on the whistle does more good than a ream of technical pamphlets. Half-way along we pass Sprey Point, an artificial platform, and Teignmouth distant. Eastcliff Bridge, and we swing away from the sea through a rock cutting into which Teignmouth station platforms extend in order to accommodate long trains like ours.

On leaving Teignmouth past the quay siding, we are beside water again, but this is the Teign estuary and we go under the 600yd road bridge to Shaldon. The cliff and furze is replaced by field and tree, past the isolated block post of Bishopsteignton by Flow Point. The sparkle changes to an ordinary muddy river amid Hackney marshes, where we shut off and coast past the sidings.

Left:
South of Sprey Point, a very mixed fast goods is caught being hauled by No 6907 *Davenham Hall*. E. D. Bruton

Devonian

Tor Bay

Newton Abbot, as its name indicates, was a piece of speculative development by the monks of Torre Abbey. It is an unremarkable market town, but to those interested in railways the name is one of those with a magical ring to it, because in 1847 the South Devon Railway established its main station and works on the flat land between the town and the Teign. Since the SDR rolling stock, like that of the Bristol & Exeter at Bridgwater, appeared to have been constructed by a bevy of inebriated blacksmiths, that may not sound very auspicious, but its importance grew over the years, it is by far the biggest employer in the district and is the pivotal point in the operation of the holiday traffic. The original workshops remain in use. Goods are handled at a depot round the corner on the Teign Valley branch and the 22-road Hackney marshalling yard, opened in 1911. The passenger station dates from 1927. Its three-storey building and 1,375ft island platforms are the archetypal Great Western station, perhaps the last flowering of an age of elegance; contrast its large but traditional signalboxes with the brick monstrosities of Bristol, erected only six years later.

As we run in, in a place of honour on the platform is seen what looks like a ceremonial tea-urn; those seeing it for the first time may be surprised to learn that it is in fact a locomotive. It is *Tiny*, built by Sara & Co of Plymouth in 1868 and used as works shunter here until 1892. It is a square platform on four wheels, with a vertical boiler and cylinders driving the wheels through gears. This is the only extant original Broad Gauge vehicle.

At the platform end a driver and fireman come over from the little hut that is the crewing nerve centre, to take over the engine. With a cheery greeting of 'The train's overweight and you've got a couple of barrows of camel s..t left to pull it', the relieved crew clear off. A cleaner from the shed climbs on to the tender to fill the tank and shovel the remaining coal forward. The supervisor is on the phone trying to get an assisting engine from somewhere, but he finally comes over to *Dumbleton Hall* to say that we will have to wait either for an engine to be brought off the shed or for one of the Torquay bankers to come up, and it will be at least 20min. The driver says he would rather go ahead, so after some more telephoning the signals are pulled off and we depart at 6.55pm. We take the relief line on the four-track section to Aller Junction, where the signalman has obtained a clear road to Torre for us. The last fireman has left a good poultice in, and the new incumbent gives it a rake through and has her blowing-off hard as his mate puts her at the bank. In accord with usual practice at junctions, an up train off the branch is scheduled at the same time, the 6.30pm Goodrington-Taunton working, and rattles briskly by as we approach the box. With everything wide open she plods steadily on at 30mph, rocking with the piston thrusts, through Kingskerswell. The fireman, fresh from his afternoon tea, ladles in plenty of coal all over the grate and is rewarded with a splendid smoke effect. Under a bridge on the main road through a cutting, over a stream and under another bridge. He puts both injectors on, the exhaust one under live steam, and drops the damper for the first time since she left Bath Road shed. Here is the summit where the line dives away at 1 in 73 through Shiphay Bridge. With the brake hard on she slows to 15mph, then rolls into Torre station to stop. The 6.30pm Kingswear-Exeter train is pounding out of the station, banked by a 2-6-2T, and when it has passed, a goods train is discovered in the up sidings: the 2.30pm from Kingswear, which has attached wagons and is now waiting for a path onwards to Hackney. Torre has extensive goods facilities, but shunting has to be done with extreme care; among the regulations, no vehicles may be left standing on the main line except in emergency, for which latter six sprags are laid out between the tracks. The reason is that beyond the platforms the line dives away at 1 in 55, apparently heading straight into the sea. To the left is Babbacombe Bay, ahead the expanse of Tor Bay with Brixham in the distance. Cautiously we ease down this incline, to stop only 66 chains further on in Torquay. This is a long station with broad platforms, several wide entrances and an extensive forecourt each side to handle the huge summer crowds. Between the platforms is a siding for the engines that bank trains up to Shiphay Bridge; there are no goods facilities.

The Tor Bay resorts form, as often found, a complementary pair. Torquay is genteel where Paignton is brash. What they share is a sheltered location, for the bay is part of a huge sweeping curve of coastline from Start Point to Portland Bill, and this gives it a climate that allows subtropical palm trees to be grown. The gardens have a Mediterranean air and, if you dislike the pier and prom, there are numerous secluded coves. That lyrical writer S. P. B. Mais claims that these face all points of the compass, but he may have been overdoing it a little. These delights are, however, hidden from the railway as it runs in a cutting until emerging on Hollacombe cliff with the gas works on the right and Gas House Siding box perched precariously over a sheer drop on the cliff edge. Paignton, where we unload the last of our holidaymakers, is equipped with a pier opened in 1879 and was then a raucous place where ladies and gentlemen took to bathing from the same beach. Even Mr Mais finds little good to say of it and admits that it lacks trees and hills. The beach also has a drawback in that the red stone so famous for Devon cliffs, when ground down to sand, becomes a brickish brown colour which is not especially enticing.

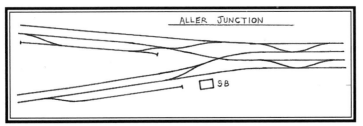

ALLER JUNCTION

SB

Below:
Pannier tank No 8466 shunts coaches at the up end of Newton Abbot on 19 July 1958. The decision to use mechanical signalling and wooden boxes in the 1927 station was an afterthought, but proved to be a wise one.
R. C. Riley

Above:
Midway between Newton Abbot and Aller Junction on 12 November 1955 is No 4936 *Kinlet Hall* on the relief line with the 11.40am Newton Abbot-Kingswear service. On the fast line is the 5.30am Paddington-Penzance express hauled by something new: BR Standard Class 7 No 70019 *Lightning.*
P. W. Gray

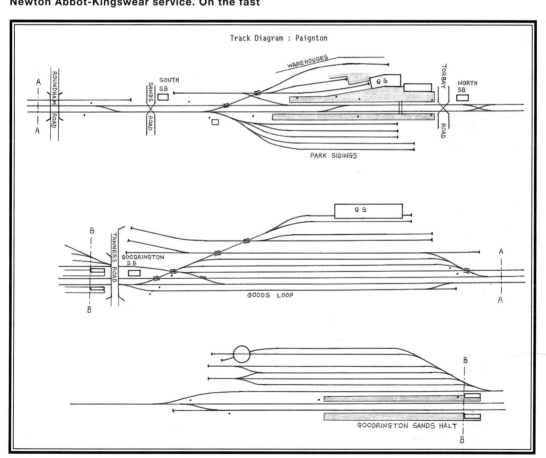

Track Diagram : Paignton

Since Paignton is just a shade anti-climactic to end our journey, we suggest staying with the empty stock for its Friday evening trip down to Kingswear. Before doing so we at last receive instructions to get rid of those two extra coaches. Since the Park Sidings are full the South signalman decides to put them in the goods yard, which nowadays serves only as a parcels depot. A shunter is standing by to do the uncoupling. We have to wait for the 7.20pm Goodrington-Plymouth service to pass (this train reverses at Newton) before shunting across and returning to the train. While this is going on assistance arrives in the form of another '5101' class 2-6-2T No 5164, which has been working the Kingswear coal trains. Coal is imported from Yorkshire for both general use and Torquay Gas Works and when a ship comes in six trainloads are worked up the branch. On this occasion the last load of the day has been left at Churston refuge siding while the engine came back to Paignton. By the time she is hitched on our front and we are ready to start it is nearly 7.35pm and the 7.20pm Kingswear-Exeter train, which we should have crossed at Churston, has been admitted to the Churston-Goodrington single line section, so although we are signalled away Goodrington has its distant on. We work slowly out of Paignton, under Roundham bridge and past the sidings, packed full with coaching stock ready for the Saturday scramble. More carriage sidings and a turntable lie behind Goodrington Sands halt, a new facility completed last summer. On the down side close by the bank cut out of Roundham Head, is a goods loop, so called, which is where the 'Devonian' set is stabled during the rest of the week. Here we shut off and our vacuum gauge needle moves as the tank engine driver puts the brake on to stop opposite Goodrington box for the token. The up train comes in, makes a brief stop and accelerates past us. After a pause our signals clear, the signalman walks across from the box and hands us a token, and both drivers open up for a rousing start. If this had been a public train we would not have stopped at the box but have run into the platform. To save the signalman walking the length of the platform a token instrument and a telephone to the box are provided in a hut at the far end, to be operated by train crews.

Off the down points at Goodrington we are straight into the 1 in 71 grade. A sea view opens out once more as we climb past Saltern Cove, Oyster Cove and Broad Sands, and turn away from the coast to cross the two lanes leading down to Broad Sands on viaducts: Broadsands and the much larger Hookhill. The sight of a long double-headed express train snaking round the bends of a steeply graded single-track branch line is an unusual one in this country and must have inspired numerous model railway owners. Any locomotive you like can run to Kingswear, since it was upgraded to 'Double Red' weight classification in 1928 and is one of the few routes cleared for the 'King' class.

Under Bascombe Road and we arrive at Churston, junction for the short Brixham branch, worked by a rail motor, ie a '14xx' class tank engine with a push-pull coach, called the 'Brixham Whippet'. Here No 5164 is detached, to return to her coal wagons. However, when she is out of the way the signalman comes to tell us that they have decided to let the 8pm Kingswear-Newton service up, rather than risk delaying it, so we settle down to wait. Now of course the train that should cross with the 8pm here is the 3.30pm through train from Paddington, which was running about five minutes late and is now standing at Paignton. Which of the two is to be allowed through the Churston-Goodrington section first is another decision for the signalmen. The fireman looks to see if he has any fire left, and in truth there is not much, so he puts some more on and runs the injector for long enough to stop her blowing-off.

At 8.10pm the up train appears and the signalman takes the token back into his box to put it in the instrument and clear the section. He pulls off our signal, comes out and hands the same token to us. After getting the train under way, drifting steam is all that is needed on the downhill run past Brim Hill to Greenway Tunnel. This is a substantial piece of work, 495yd long; its southern end breaks out into a steep, wooded valley, crossed by the 150yd Maypool Viaduct. (Indeed, the very name of Devon is derived from the Celtic *Dyfnaint*, meaning 'dark and deep valleys'.) The descent is taken with caution, as the speed limit is 30mph from Goodrington to Noss curve, 35mph from there to Britannia halt and 40mph thence to Kingswear. Coming out of the tunnel, the River Dart appears ahead, tranquil between its tree-

Right:
Aller Junction in May 1955: No 7909 *Heveningham Hall* is hauling a local from Plymouth; the first coach is one of the 1935 'Centenary' stock. Note the traffic on the main Torquay road in the background. *H. Gordon Tidey*

Below:
On the Torbay branch, nearing Kingskerswell, No 4969 *Shrugborough Hall* is at the head of the 1.25pm from Paddington at about 5.45pm on 14 July 1956. *D. J. Fish*

Left:
On a summer morning in 1957 the up 'Devonian' is assisted out of Paignton by 2-6-2T No 4105. The train engine is No 6982 *Melmerby Hall.* Ian Allan Library

Centre left:
In the evening of 30 March 1962, the 2.30pm Paddington-Kingswear service starts away from Paignton. The 2-6-2T No 5153 is especially clean because attached to the train is a Royal Train saloon carrying Princess Margaret on a visit to Torquay.
Ian Allan Library

Below left:
On 21 July 1962, seen from Roundham Road bridge, 'King' No 6018 *King Henry VI* has brought a down train into Paignton and is drawing the empty coaches into the carriage sidings. The engine has worked tender-first from Newton Abbot in readiness to take out an up express.
Ian Allan Library

Above right:
With postwar development creeping down the hill from the main road, 2-6-2T No 5108 crosses Hookhill Viaduct on the climb away from Tor Bay. Behind her is a distant signal, fixed permanently at Caution since all trains must slow to 15mph to change single-line tokens at Churston. R. E. Toop

Right:
An excursion special from Bristol, hauled by No 6981 *Marbury Hall,* rounds the Noss deviation above buildings of Philip's shipyard, on 8 September 1957. Passengers in the non-corridor coaches may well be relieved to see journey's end.
D. J. Fish

clad slopes and glowing in the evening light. Down we go, adjusting the brake to hold her steady until we are beside the water, its cool silence juxtaposed with and emphasised by *Dumbleton Hall's* heat and the ringing of her rods. She swings away on a curved embankment taking her inland round Noss Point; a later alteration completed in 1923, the line originally crossed the point by means of two viaducts. Past a steeply-graded siding leading down into Noss Shipyard, we rejoin the waterside and come to Britannia Halt, a little wooden platform next to the ferry slipway. Giving her steam once more, we gather speed along the level. On our left the long Hoodown Siding is occupied by a spotless rake of chocolate and cream liveried coaches: the stock of the 'Torbay Express', the crack train of these parts. Across the water, Dartmouth is to some extent obscured by the bulk of moored ships, but if you know where to look you may spot its station — the unique station which has no railway, where passengers commence their journey by boat. The river is taken for granted as a highway here, for were it not for the ferries, Dartmouth would be over 25 miles by road from Kingswear.

Kingswear station is built on an artificial platform which has been progressively extended over the years, the last time in 1932 when the coal cranes were installed. The carriage sidings are also on infilled ground, constructed in 1929. Before the railway came the ground sloped down from Fore Street into the water. Now the quay is silent, its sidings cleared of wagons and the collier *Similarity* riding high and empty at her moorings, ready to leave. The signalman stops us at his home signal, then lowers it and leans out of the box to shout 'Run round' as we pass. The driver accordingly stops clear of the points at the far end of the platform. A porter-signalman unlocks the ground frame operating these points while our fireman uncouples the engine and we draw forward into the wooden roof at the end of the line. Backing out, we run past the coaches and pull up opposite the box. A few minutes later the London train comes in, turning into the other platform face. It is half-past eight, the light is fading from behind the headlands down the harbour, and already it looks quite dark up Waterhead Creek. The fireman lights the headlamps which he has taken off the front, hangs one on the

centre bottom lamp bracket on the tender, and places the other, with its red shade turned down, back on the front.

There is still a lot of activity at Kingswear; three arrivals and three departures are yet to come, and after the shunting is complete ready for the morning and the engines sent away, Paignton receives its last arrival at midnight and despatches a sleeper to London, then there is only a few hours' break before the Saturday rush begins. But it is true that *Dumbleton Hall* has very little coal left in her tender, so we will send her back light to Newton shed for servicing. The night will be far advanced by the time she has been coaled, watered and examined, for they have about 50 engines to get ready. Squads of men are hard at work emptying smokeboxes, raking out ashpans, cleaning tubes, cleaning paint and brasswork, filling oil bottles, drying sand, counting out corks and sponge cloths, and all the other jobs that keep the wheels turning. It is time to leave them to it. Above the lap of the ever-moving tide comes a single short whistle as the engine approaches Steam Ferry Crossing. The air-pump spits and the ring of her rods fades, and a banner of white steam traces her along the dark shore until it vanishes among the trees.

Below:
On an evening in 1951, 'Castle' No 7000 *Viscount Portal* drifts into Kingswear with through coaches from Liverpool, past a derelict lighter and the Torbay stock in its usual berth on Hoodown siding. The distant signal showing Clear does not mean a collision is imminent, merely that the crossing at Britannia Halt is open.
Ian Allan Library

Above:
On the morning of 2 October 1958, No 6012
King Edward VI is turned on the Kingswear
turntable. With Waterhead Creek as a background, this is arguably the most beautiful
setting in the country for a railway scene.
Ian Allan Library

Below:
The up 'Devonian' labours up the 1 in 75 past
Brim Hill on its way from Kingswear to
Churston on a Saturday morning in 1956. The
locomotive is No 5024 *Carew Castle*.
D. J. Fish

Above:
At Churston on a July Saturday in 1956, 'Castle' No 4088 *Dartmouth Castle* is a happy choice of power for the up 'Devonian'. In the station, through the arches of the Kingswear road bridge, are the rear of what will be the 9.45am working to Paddington, and the 'Brixham Whippet'. *D. J. Fish*

Left:
After the Paignton-Kingswear line was taken over by a private company and run as the Torbay Railway, it hosted the occasional through excursion from London. Ex-GWR 2-6-2T No 4588 and pannier tank No 6412 stand at Kingswear on one such on 15 April 1973. The platform and run-round were the only tracks remaining at that time. *SHA*

Above:
A view over Kingswear station up the Dart in a later era, on 2 April 1983. Besides the curtailment of the railway, another difference from **the 1950s is the mass of expensive boats. The train is the Venice Simplon Orient-Express on an excursion from London.**
SHA

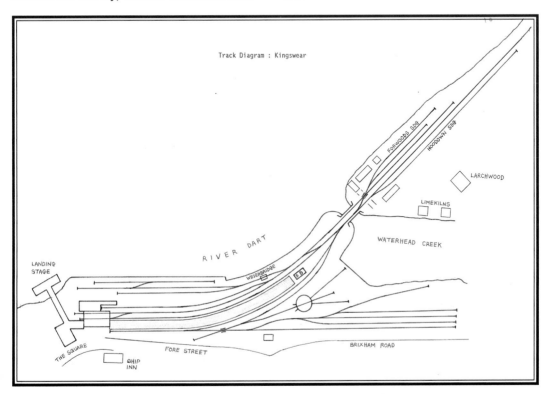

Track Diagram : Kingswear

Conclusion

There is no intention in these pages to instigate comparisons between the railways of 1957 and those of any other time. However, we assume that the reader is more interested in the railway as a varied community of people serving the wider community on every scale from the mass to the individual, than in it as a piece of high technology, so we will conclude with a few notes on where the spirit of the 'Devonian' may still be found.

On the route the major civil engineering works are still in place, and such sights as the stonework of the Anker Viaduct in Tamworth or the plunge over the edge of the Lickey Incline are still worth seeing for their own sakes. At Bristol Temple Meads the overall roof and main entrance are magnificently preserved, and Sheffield Midland retains much of its character, but for the details that make up the true railway environment we have to thank the 'Heritage' railways. The Keighley & Worth Valley Railway is a Midland branch line and has many items typical of that company, including the original Frizinghall signalbox. The Torbay & Dartmouth Railway is actually the Paignton-Kingswear line, but it is only fair to acknowledge that it is run on commercial lines and is virtually a new railway on the site of the old one. The goods yards and sidings were lost before they could be preserved, and with a new station on the site of the Queens Park sidings, Paignton is possibly unique among stations used by British Railways in having more passenger accommodation now than at any time in the past. However, Goodrington signalbox is still where it was in 1957 and still controlling steam-hauled trains as it did then. The Midland Railway has an establishment devoted to its memory, appropriately located near Derby, at Butterley on the branch line between Ambergate and Pye Bridge. The Great Western Railway has its centre at Didcot. It is also appropriate to mention that the Middleton Railway, true to its premier status, became the first standard gauge railway to be run by a voluntary society and,

Below:
The '5X' selected for preservation from those running in 1967 was No 5593 *Kolhapur*. She is seen here in Holbeck shed while still in British Railways ownership. *Ian Allan Library*

wearing its historical significance lightly, carries on working amid drastically altered surroundings.

Of the locomotives, no Stanier 2-6-2T has survived, but Class 2MT No 41241 runs on the Keighley & Worth Valley Railway. No 45407 is one of many '5P5Fs' still running; she was preserved by Mr Paddy Smith and, while nominally based at Steamtown, Carnforth, has travelled widely on the main lines. *Alberta* was not preserved, as a group set up to save one of the last '5Xs' chose No 45593 *Kolhapur* as the best prospect. The latter is now on the Great Central Railway which, at the time of writing, is probably the best place to see steam trains in a main line ambience, although that could change with such developments as the Peak Railway (which is on the route of a former Midland main line). *Leander* was rescued from a scrapyard and rebuilt by the firm of Oliver, Taylor & Crossley Ltd, and has also been an outstanding performer on BR excursions. One of the '94xx' series taper-boiler pannier tanks, No 9466, is owned by Mr Dennis Howells and her home base is the Buckinghamshire Railway Centre at Quainton Road station. Great Western 2-6-2Ts may be found at several places: No 4160 runs on the West Somerset Railway and No 5164 is on the Severn Valley Railway, where you may also find the mixture of GW, LMS and BR coaches that formed the Midlands-West Country trains of the 1950s. *Dumbleton Hall* is one of seven 'Halls' preserved, rebuilt from scrapyard state by the Dumbleton Hall Preservation Society. She has returned to service on the Torbay & Dartmouth Railway, where the trains of the 1990s are as close in resemblance to those of the 1950s, or the 1930s for that matter, as any in the country. And of course we should not forget *Tiny*; she is in the South Devon Railway museum at Buckfastleigh.

What is of prime importance is that at all the locations mentioned the trains are seen together with all sorts of other equipment and furnishings, functioning in the context of a complete operating railway. Obviously they are not 'authentic', for no small firm or voluntary group can hope to reproduce the sidings of Cudworth, or Newton Abbot in full blast on a summer Saturday; what they are creating is not the stasis of museums but living community railways for the 21st century; a greater challenge. The fact that much of the inspiration, finance and hard labour has come from volunteers — amateurs in the finest sense of the word — makes their achievement all the more remarkable. They are worthy successors to those men, of the very highest calibre this society has produced, whose work is praised in this book.

Below:
A pair of '5P5Fs' moving past the magnificent Midland Railway station of Hellifield, to work the 'Cumbrian Mountain Express' on 4 April 1981 to Carlisle. Both have reverted to LMS numbers; the leading one is No 4767, the rear one is No 5407. *SHA*

Appendix

A list of Signal Boxes

Bradford Forster Square Station
Manningham Sta.
Manningham Sidings
Frizinghall Sta.
Shipley Goods Sidings
Shipley Bradford Junction
Shipley Leeds Jn.
Guiseley Jn.
Thackley Jn.
Apperley Viaduct
Apperley Bridge Sta.
Apperley Jn.
Calverley & Rodley
Newlay & Horsforth
Kirkstall Jn.
Armley Canal Road No 2 (SL only)
Armley Canal Road No 1 (SL only)
Wortley Jn.
Whitehall Jn.
Leeds City North Jn.
Wellington
Engine Shed Jn.
Hunslet Goods Jn.
Hunslet Station Jn.
Hunslet South Jn.
Hunslet Wakefield Road
Stourton Jn.
Rothwell Haigh
Waterloo Colliery Sidings
Woodlesford Sta.
Methley North Sidings
Methley North Jn.
            IBS
Altofts
Normanton North
Normanton Passenger Station North
Normanton Passenger Station South
Normanton Goose Hill
St. Johns Colliery Siding
Snydale
Oakenshaw North
Oakenshaw South
West Riding Jn.
            IBS
Royston & Notton Jn.

Hodroyd's & Monckton Main Sidings
Royston Sta.
Carlton Main Sidings
Cudworth North Jn.
Cudworth South Jn.
Cudworth Sta.
Storrs Mill Jn.
Houghton Colliery Sidings
Dearne Valley Colliery Sdgs GL only
Darfield Sta.
Wath North North
Wath North Sta.
Manvers Main Colliery Sdgs
Wath Road Jn.
Swinton Town Jn.
Swinton Town Sta.
Kilnhurst West South Sta.
Roundwood
Rawmarsh Sta.
Parkgate Jn.
Masborough Station North
Masborough Station South Jn.
Holmes Jn.
Harrison & Camms Sidings
Wincobank North Jn.
Wincobank Station Jn.
Brightside Station Jn.
Upwell Street Jn.
Grimesthorpe Jn. No 1
Mill Race Jn.
Nunnery Main Line Jn.
Sheffield North Jn.
Sheffield Station B (Up & p5 only)
Sheffield South No 2 (Up only)
Queens Road
Heeley Sta.
Heeley Carriage Sidings
Millhouses Sta.
Beauchief Sta.
Dore & Totley Station Jn.
Dore & Totley South Jn.
Dronfield Colliery Sidings
Dronfield Sta.
Unstone Colliery Sidings
            IBS

Tapton Jn.
Chesterfield North
Chesterfield Sta.
Chesterfield (Midland) South
Horns Bridge
Hollis Lane (GL only)
Hasland Sidings
Clay Cross North Jn.
Clay Cross South Jn.
Stretton
        IBS
Shirland Sidings
Wingfield Sta.
Crich Jn.
Ambergate North Jn.
Ambergate South Jn.
Broadholme
Belper Goods
Duffield Jn.
Peckwash Mill Sidings
Little Eaton Jn.
Breadsall Crossing
St. Mary's Jn.
Derby North Jn.
Derby Jn.
Derby Station North Jn.
Derby A
London Road Jn.
L.N.W. Jn.
Melbourne Jn.
Sunny Hill Jn.
Stenson Jn.
Repton & Willington Sta.
        IBS
Clay Mills Jn.
Wetmore Sidings
North Stafford Jn.
Horninglow Bridge
Burton Station North
Burton Station South
Leicester Jn.
Branston Jn.
        IBS
Barton & Walton Sta.
Wichnor Jn.
Wichnor Sidings
        IBS
Elford
        IBS No 1
        IBS No 2
Tamworth High Level
Kettlebrook Sidings
Wilnecote, Perrin & Harrison's Sidings
Whateley Sidings
Cliff Sidings
Kingsbury Branch Sidings
Kingsbury Station Jn.

Water Orton Station Jn.
Water Orton Jn.
Castle Bromwich Jn.
Bromford Bridge
Washwood Heath Jn.
Washwood Heath Sidings No 1
Saltley Sidings
Saltley Jn.
Duddeston Road
Landor Street Jn.
Curzon Street Grand Jn.
Proof House Jn.
New Street No 2
New Street No 4
New Street No 5
Church Road Jn.
Selly Oak Sta.
Bournville Sta.
Kings Norton Station Jn.
Northfield Sta.
Halesowen Jn.
Barnt Green Main Line Jn.
Blackwell Sta.
Bromsgrove Sta.
Bromsgrove South
Stoke Works Jn.
Dunhampstead
Spetchley
Abbots Wood Jn.
Pirton Sidings
Defford Sta.
Eckington Sta.
Bredon Sta.
Ashchurch Sta.
Cleeve Sta.
Cheltenham High Street
Alston Jn.
Cheltenham Lansdown Sta.
Lansdown Jn.
Hatherley Jn.
Churchdown
Elm Bridge
Engine Shed Jn.
Tramway Jn.
Gloucester North
Gloucester South Jn.
Tuffley Jn.
Naas Crossing
Haresfield
Standish Jn.
Stonehouse Bristol Road
Frocester
Coaley Jn.
Berkeley Road Jn.
Berkeley Road South Jn.
Wick
Charfield

Wickwar
Rangeworthy
Yate Main Line Jn.
Yate South Jn.
Westerleigh North Jn.
Westerleigh South Jn.
Shortwood Sidings
Mangotsfield North Jn.
Mangotsfield Station Jn.
Staple Hill
Fishponds
Kingswood Jn.
Lawrence Hill Jn.
Engine Shed Sidings
Bristol Temple Meads East
Bristol Temple Meads Old Sta.
Bath Road Locomotive Yard
Bristol Temple Meads West
Bedminster Sta.
Malago Vale
Parson Street Jn.
West Depot
South Liberty Jn.
IBS
Flax Bourton
Nailsea & Backwell
Claverham
Yatton East
Yatton West
Huish Crossing
Puxton & Worle
Worle Jn.
Hutton
Weston-super-Mare
Uphill Jn.
Lympsham
Brent Knoll
Highbridge North
Highbridge Crossing
Huntspill
Pottery Siding
Dunball
Bridgwater
Meads Crossing
Fordgate
Durston
Cogload
Creech Jn.
Taunton East Jn.
Taunton West Sta.
Taunton West Jn.
Taunton East Loop
Taunton West Loop
Silkmill Crossing
Norton Fitzwarren
Victory Siding
Poole Siding

Wellington
IBS
Whiteball Tunnel
Burlescombe
Sampford Peverell
Tiverton Jn.
Cullompton
Westcott
Hele & Bradninch
Silverton
Rewe
Stoke Canon Crossing
Stoke Canon Jn.
Cowley Bridge Jn.
Exeter Riverside
Exeter East
Exeter Middle
Exeter West
Exeter St Thomas
City Basin Jn.
Cotfield
Exminster
Powderham
Starcross
Dawlish Warren
Dawlish
Parson's Tunnel
Teignmouth
Old Quay
Bishopsteignton
Hackney
Newton Abbot East
Newton Abbot West
Aller Jn.
Kingskerswell
Torre
Torquay
Gas House Siding
Paignton North
Paignton South
Goodrington
Churston
Kingswear
Yate-Bristol via WR
Westerleigh North Jn.
Westerleigh West Jn.
Coalpit Heath
Winterbourne
Stoke Gifford East
Stoke Gifford West
Filton Jn.
Filton Incline
Ashley Hill
Stapleton Road
Lawrence Hill
Dr Day's Bridge Jn.
Bristol Temple Meads East